POLITICAL JOURNALISM: NEW CHALLENGES

M.S. Bisht

CYBER TECH PUBLICATIONS
4264/3, Ansari Road, Daryaganj, New Delhi-110002 (India)
Ph.: 011-23244078. Fax: 011-23280028
E-Mail: cyberpublicationsdelhi@yahoo.com

POLITICAL JOURNALISM: NEW CHALLENGES

M.S. Bisht

First Edition 2009

Reprint: 2026

Published by :

G.S. Rawat for Cyber Tech Publications
4264/3, Ansari Road, Daryaganj, New Delhi-110002 (India)
Ph.: 011-23244078. Fax: 011-23280028
E-Mail: cyberpublicationsdelhi@yahoo.com

Printed at : **Amit Enterprises**, Maujpur, Delhi, (9810878184)

Preface

In countries where freedom of the press is not restricted, the media can adopt three main positions in their relationship to political parties and politicians. The first is to serve as loyal channels for particular parties and politicians, acting as reliable partners and enabling them to exercise a high degree of control over their political messages. Parties in such a position can feel sure that their political message will reach the voters and that their positions will be defended in the struggle for their favour. The second position is for the media to function as an independent arena, making broadcasting time and column space available to political actors of different shades of opinion. Neutral media of this kind place greater demands on the communicative skills of the politicians, in a political terrain in which none have protection against unfavourable comment and all are without permanent allies.

This book deals with all the technicalities and procedures of Political Journalism, I Hope that readers will find it of great benefit for themselves.

—Author

CONTENTS

1

POLITICAL JOURNALISM THE ZIMBABWEAN WAY

INTRODUCTION

The situation ahead of Zimbabwe's fifth parliamentary election in 2000 was in two important ways different from the former elections held in the country since the independence from Ian Smith's Rhodesia in 1980.

First, for the first time a serious opponent challenged ZANU PF and President Robert Mugabe: Movement for Democratic Change (MDC), led by Morgan Tsvangirai, and established as late as in September 1999. As a nationally unified party, MDC had a sufficiently broad social and ethnic base to present a serious challenge to ZANU PF, and the party quickly attracted widespread support. Mugabe's defeat in the mid-February referendum on the new draft constitution clearly demonstrated that the election result in the coming parliamentary election should not be taken for granted (Saunders 2001).

Secondly, in the late 1990s ZANU PF had lost their former full control of the media (Rønning & Kupe 2000; Saunders 2000; Rønning 2003). Although ZANU PF still controlled both radio and TV organised in Zimbabwe Broadcasting Corporation (ZBC) and the titles within Zimpapers, the editorial policy of the weeklies The Zimbabwe

Independent and The Standard, both launched in 1996-97, and The Daily News launched in 1999, were all strongly opposed to the established regime of ZANU PF.

This new situation did not, however, lead to a competition on equal terms between ZANU PF and the MDC, neither on the political scene nor on the media scene. Concerning the political aspects of the election campaign ZANU PF had some clear advantages.

The party was well known to the voters, it had a glorious history from the independence war, and it had complete control of the state apparatus. The MDC had as a new party, no historical past, the voters had not yet gained the same knowledge of the party leadership, and the party did not receive any support from the state bureaucracy. Concerning the media both radio and TV served as a propaganda channel for ZANU PF, more or less ignoring MDC (Zaffiro 2002).

The support to the two political rivals from the newspapers was more equal, at least in Harare where The Daily News was more or less a match for the state-controlled daily The Herald. The pro-opposition weeklies had, however, nothing like as many readers as the state-controlled The Sunday Mail. An election in which two parties were campaigning against each other, both with media supporting their politics, created a much more open political situation in Zimbabwe than before.

The question in this paper is what consequences this openness had for the election campaign and for the struggle for power between the ruling regime and their new challenger. Or more precisely: In which way did the new media situation influence the election campaign agenda? What kind of information did the voters get from the media about the coming election? How did the media depict the two rivalling political parties, and their leading politicians?

The analysis builds on my book Politics and Persuasion, Media coverage of Zimbabwe's 2000 election (Waldahl 2004), and spans the period from the referendum on the new draft constitution in mid-February to one week after the election on 24 and 25 June. Within this period, I have analysed News@eight, the main TV news programme from ZBC, as well as the main newspapers in Zimbabwe.

The study is based on a qualitative analysis of all relevant items in ZBC's News@eight, and of election-related articles in the newspapers. On that basis, I have defined important characteristics of the media's coverage of the campaign, and compared their treatments of major political issues. Such a strategy does not give a precise picture of quantitative aspects, but does illuminate special features of the political contents of the media, and place the news items in a wider context.

THE ELECTION CAMPAIGN AGENDA

Political influence is to a large extent dependent on the ability of politicians to put their pet causes on the political agenda, focusing voter attention on areas where they stand to make political gains (Dearing & Rogers 1996; McCombs 2004). In modern society this can only be done with the assistance of the media. Matters given priority by the media appear more important than matters to which they pay little attention, and politicians rarely win a public hearing for their favourite causes if they do not arouse media interest. The focus the media give particular social problems is therefore important for the criteria on which the voters base their assessments of political life and its actors (Iyengar & Kinder 1987; Willnat 1997). This means that problems that attract wide media attention will be those of which voters are most aware when they make their political choices, and which most likely will figure prominently in their assessments of parties and politicians.

In an election where the political debate is marked by questions of foreign policy, voters will assess parties and politicians principally according to their supposed ability to maintain the country's foreign policy interests, whereas their economic qualifications will count for most if the election is marked by an economic crisis. In all political systems some parties will have a special ownership to certain issues, and a party holding a dominant position towards an important issue at the political agenda will have an obvious advantage compared to their rival parties (Petrocik 1996). In terms of this ownership theory, ZANU PF based their election strategy on two old issues which had been the cornerstones of the success of the party from the independence war and onwards. These two issues - intended to secure the ruling party's renewed confidence among the electorate - were the question of who was to own the land, and the struggle against unwarranted intervention in the country's internal affairs by the former colonial power, Great Britain.

President Mugabe and the other party leaders proclaimed this message forcefully, and the pro-government media followed up loyally by emphasising those two issues throughout the campaign. Neither ZBC nor the newspapers within Zimpapers paid much attention to the many serious challenges facing Zimbabwe in the new millennium: an inflation rate at 60 per cent, more than half of the work force unemployed, some 60 per cent of the people living below the poverty line and a serious HIV/AIDS problem decreasing the life expectancy for new-born infants to less than 40 years.

Mugabe's tactics were successful. Neither the MDC nor the pro-opposition media managed to establish an alternative agenda on which to base attacks against ZANU PF's weak spots, and they did not note that Mugabe was looking back rather than forward in his selection of campaign issues. The pro-opposition newspapers stressed however from time to time that Mugabe had had twenty years in which to redistribute the land without achieving significant results, and that Great Britain could hardly be said to be a real threat to the country's independence. However, none of the two arguments was put forward strongly and systematically, and the pro-opposition press did not seriously confront ZANU PF on its two core campaign issues.

Thus, although the ZANU PF strategy looks likes a gift to an opposition party willing and able to confront the serious problems facing Zimbabwe, the MDC did not exploit this possibility. From the point of view of the country's circumstances, the time was certainly ripe for political change. ZANU PF had succeeded in the struggle to free the country from white minority government, but it was now apparent that the party had neither the will nor the ability to adopt a forward-looking policy for the benefit of the people. A party showing their intention to take hold of these problems should have a good chance of doing well in the election.

The MDC did not take the challenge, and the pro-oppositional newspapers did not give the party any help by directing the voter's attention towards such questions. There was no media debate on the reasons for high unemployment and inflation or on what it would take to stimulate the country's economy. Little was heard about measures that might slow down the spread of HIV/AIDS or what could be done for those already suffering its consequences. True enough, commentary articles in the pro-opposition papers occasionally addressed these issues, but in the struggle for public opinion they virtually vanished. Nor did the pro-opposition media devote much attention to Zimbabwe's military engagement in the Congo, which should have been a good cause for them to take up, in view of its impact on the country's economy.

This does not, however, mean that the election campaign agenda was completely dominated by ZANU PF's agenda. The pro-oppositional media also contributed to the agenda, but their focus was primarily on the incidence of politically motivated violence and on the question of whether the election was properly conducted.

The first of these two questions was to a certain degree a theme also in the pro-government media, but in quite another way (MMPZ 2000). The second theme was almost completely absent in these media, and without the media that were beyond state control, the question of whether irregularities had taken place in the conduct of the election would not have been raised. And if it not had been, the issue of the legitimacy of the election would not have acquired the significance that it did. The opposition and their media allies were thus not without some influence on the election campaign agenda.

Their spin on the political violence and their emphasis on the conduct of the election widened the campaign perspective and drew attention to aspects of it that, were it not for them, would have passed by in silence. This helped to show the voters that the election was about more than the practical solutions to concrete problems; it was also about the respect of the parties for popular opinion and their willingness to compete for their votes by honest means. The voters were thus given a broader set of criteria on which to base their choice between the parties.

The campaign strategies put forward by the two main opponents and their media allies led to an election campaign marked by two different agendas. One related to substantial political issues, another to the conduct of the election campaign. On the one hand could the pro-governmental media, unchallenged by an alternative oppositional agenda, campaign for the implementation of ZANU PF's land reform and for a defence against British imperialism. On the other hand, did the pro-opposition newspapers make significant contributions to the agenda through the attention they gave to the formal aspects of the election campaign and to the methods used by the government?

These are questions which neither the ZBC nor newspapers within Zimpapers cared much about. The result was a campaign where the two parties did not in any real sense confront each other, and where the main politicians from the two parties did not debate each other neither in the media nor in public. It also meant that the question of whether irregularities had taken place in the conduct of the election would not have been raised without the media that were beyond state control. And in that case, the issue of the legitimacy of the election would not have acquired the significance that it did.

INFORMING THE VOTERS

Modern media are society's major source of political knowledge. It is not possible for voters to form considered opinions on political issues without relevant and credible information from the media, and according to liberal theory, media should act as an information agency facilitating the functioning of democracy (Curran 2002, 225).

In order to carry out this duty, the media must recognise their social responsibilities and put the voters first. In a democratic society, there is an obligation on the media to help the voters to take well-founded decisions on political issues. The media's information work has two main aspects. The first aspect concerns the media's obligation to provide facts on the procedures for implementing the election, and to inform the voters about their rights and duties in that connection. This includes the information needed to enable voters to cast valid votes, and is especially important in societies where the general level of political knowledge is low. On the other hand, the media have to provide information concerning the political alternatives on offer and draw attention to the politicians who are fighting for them.

This is a complex task. The media must draw attention to the questions that have a bearing on people's living conditions, explain the views held by the political parties on these questions, and show what effects various solutions may have. They must also describe society's most important cleavages and relate the political parties to them. For voters who want to exercise their civic rights and take part in the elections, there are many details to keep track of concerning the election proceedings and their formal rights as citizens. In the political climate prevailing prior to the 2000 election, there was one more question of special relevance to the Zimbabwean electorate. Could one be certain that the ballot really was secret, or was there a risk of someone discovering how one voted? Both this contextually based question and the more ordinary but nevertheless important questions are what people need to know the answers to before casting their votes. They are, however, questions, which the Zimbabwean media did little to answer.

Two problems arise when considering how the media fulfilled their duties in this respect. One is that some of the information given was inaccurate, making it difficult for voters to know what precisely to make of it. This was both true in terms of the election date, concerning which the media carried unclear and partly contradictory information right up to the middle of May, and in terms of when voter registration was to terminate, which the media failed to clarify unanimously or unambiguously. Confusion of this nature, however, could only be partly blamed on the media, since the authorities themselves were unclear and indecisive on these points. Where issues of such importance are concerned, however, the media should not have rested as content as they demonstrably did, but should instead have spotlighted the problems, and challenged the authorities.

The second problem was that information given by the media on many of these questions was either inadequate or non-existent, and appeared only sporadically. Voters with concrete questions rarely found their answers in the media. What all this adds up to is that the media provided the voters with far too little information on the election arrangements and on the steps voters had to take to perform their civic duty at the election. Such voter education is particularly important in a country like Zimbabwe, where sectors of the population know too little about these matters. The obligation to provide voters with such information should be felt equally by all media. The state-controlled media should have considered it their duty to serve as mediators for the authorities, to prevent lack of knowledge from limiting voters' opportunities to take part in the election. The media that were hoping for a political change in the country should for their part have considered it important to ensure that insufficient knowledge did not prevent a change. Neither of them performed that job in a satisfactory way. The other information-related aspect concerns the media's effort to give the voters a foundation for carefully considered choices between the competing candidates, and in that way to acquaint the voters with the political parties, and with their policies.

In election campaigns prominent politicians will appear both in the general news and in campaign reporting in particular. In the regular news, edited according to general journalistic criteria, politicians in leading positions always have an advantage over those in less prominent roles, especially in countries where news mediation adheres to a strongly elitist tradition. Zimbabwe is such a country, and it is not surprising that Mugabe in particular, but also other

ZANU PF politicians, figured much more prominently in the news than the leading opposition politicians. Mugabe's exposure was, as one should imagine, especially marked in the ZBC and the newspaper within Zimpapers, but The Daily News and the pro-opposition weeklies also paid considerable attention to Mugabe.

Nevertheless, neither he nor the other leading ZANU PF politicians were as dominant there as in the pro-government media, mainly because they carried more material on the MDC, resulting in a better balance between government and opposition politicians. There is, however, no doubt that Mugabe had much more media exposure than his main competitor Tsvangirai, and that he outshone him in apparent importance.

The imbalances were at least as great, and generally along the same dividing lines, in the way the media presented the election campaign and the parties' preparations for the election. In this respect, too, the ZBC stood out as the warmest media adherent to ZANU PF. It is beyond doubt that, in the eyes of the ZBC, only one party deserved attention before the 2000 election. The pro-government newspaper also showed distinctly pro-ZANU PF and anti-MDC profiles, and although the bias was not as obvious as in the ZBC, their political profiles defined them as solid supporters of Mugabe and his party.

The pro-opposition newspapers were differently placed. Both The Daily News and the privately-owned weeklies devoted much greater attention than the pro-government media to the activities of the MDC and its leading politicians, but it was impossible for these media to neglect the country's ruling party to the same extent as the pro-government media neglected the opposition. If they had, they would not have fulfilled their role as news media, and reduced public support would have been a likely result. Nevertheless, the pro-opposition newspapers consequently showed much less of a bias in favour of the MDC than the pro-government media did in favour of ZANU PF.

The existence of newspapers beyond the control of Zimpapers prior to the 2000 election meant a less one-sided, though far from equal, media situation for ZANU PF and the other parties. The opposition was visible in the media as it had not been before, and they managed to place their worry about the legal aspects of the accomplishment of the election on the campaign agenda. Voters looking for information on what the challengers to ZANU PF stood for were, therefore, this time able to find it, even if the difference between the media was great. Whereas the pro-opposition papers publicised both the ruling party and the opposition, and presented ZANU PF and the MDC as two more or less equivalent alternatives, the ruling party was given much more space in the pro-government media, where it was presented as the only real alternative in the election.

MEDIATED POLITICAL COMPETITION

In the 2000 election ZANU PF was, for the first time since independence, confronted with a political rival they had to take seriously. An important question in this new situation was what attitude the two main opponents would take to each other. Would they, in keeping with democratic principles, recognise each other's legitimate rights to compete for the voters' favour, and respect each other's political positions, or would the personal qualifications of the politicians, and their motives and ambitions steal most of the attention? The answer is simple; the leading media on either side in the election campaign had little praise for their counterpart's undisputed leader, Robert Mugabe and Morgan Tsvangirai. The media's characteristics were predominantly linked to their legitimacy, their skill and their honesty.

When the voters weigh up politicians that are standing for election, they must take into account which values they are fighting for and which interests are behind them. From that point of view, the pro-government media painted an unambiguous and consistent picture of the MDC and its leaders. The MDC was not a national party seeking to improve conditions for the Zimbabwean people, but an instrument in the hands of the country's white minority, who were still dreaming of a return to Ian Smith's Rhodesia, and of the British Labour Government, which wanted to re-colonise the country. The main purpose of this concentration on an alleged alliance between the MDC, the white farmers and the British was certainly to reduce the MDC's legitimacy among the voters and to question the opposition's patriotism. Could voters possibly support a party that was seeking renewed political and economic subjection to the British? ZANU PF's answer, loudly conveyed by 'their' media, was a definite 'no'. In the view of the pro-government media, and of ZANU PF, Zimbabwe had won its independence through a patriotic fight involving great sacrifice, and experience in that battle was still a prerequisite for anyone seeking a leading position in society.

There was in the eyes of ZANU PF a crucial distinction between 'us', who had contributed to the country's independence, and 'them', who had not. Political legitimacy in Zimbabwean politics was still indissolubly attached to the liberation struggle, and by that standard the MDC leadership did not measure up. The pro-opposition media were not in a position to cast similar doubts on ZANU PF's patriotic background: the effort of its leaders in the liberation struggle was an indisputable fact. Instead, they asked what use the party leadership had made of the unlimited power they had had since independence. Whose interests had they been serving in those twenty years? For these newspapers, the answer was plain and simple: chiefly their own, by securing their positions in society. According to the opposition's allies in the media, the losers, those who were bound to suffer for the leaders'-avarice, were the people, whose living conditions had clearly worsened during the 1990s. This must not continue, argued these media, and in their view the MDC would do something about it. From their point of view, the election meant a choice between the sitting government that was chiefly concerned with advancing the interests of a small powerful elite, and opposition intent on working for the benefit of the entire population. The gap was, in other words, a wide one.

According to the pro-government media, the opposition lacked not only political legitimacy, but also the skill required of the political leadership. This criticism was above all directed at Tsvangirai's personal qualifications and political experience. According to the pro-government media, Tsvangirai was not a sufficiently serious politician to measure up against ZANU PF. He did not carry the political weight needed to lead a party, not to mention the entire nation, he vacillated, he repeatedly went back on statements made in public, and even his own principal supporters were beginning to question his political skill. The message to the voters was perfectly clear: the leader of the MDC lacked the qualities expected of a top-level politician. Tsvangirai was moreover not alone, the pro-government media continued, in failing to meet the necessary standards; the party was also having serious problems in finding qualified election candidates. This view was to a high degree based on the MDCs candidate selection system which contrary to ZANU PF did not have an open nomination process. And when MDC's list finally did come out, The Herald had little praise for the nominees; most of whom they claimed were either unsuccessful politicians who had tried their hands in other parties before, or former student activists with a record of violent demonstrations.

Whereas the opposition leaders and candidates lacked political experience at the national level, making it difficult for them to refute the charge that they were lacking in political skill, the majority of the ruling party's candidates had long political careers behind them. For the pro-opposition media, this was both an advantage and a disadvantage. On the one hand, they could not accuse their opponents of lacking experience. On the other, they had plenty of opportunity to carry out critical examinations of what they had achieved as politicians.

They availed themselves less of such opportunities than one might have expected, but some assessments were made, especially relating to ZANU PF's handling of the land issue. Several times in the course of the election campaign, The Daily News and The Zimbabwe Independent noted the paradox that it was not until now, twenty years after liberation that Mugabe was grappling seriously with the land issue. Under a skilful government, land distribution would have looked very different. The pro-government and pro-opposition media attacked their opponents' political skills from different perspectives. The pro-government media looked ahead, spotlighted the politicians who were challenging the ruling party, and concluded that they did not have the personal qualifications needed to lead the country. The pro-opposition media were more inclined to look back, and to consider the country's situation in important areas, before establishing that the ruling politicians had not done a good enough job. On the whole, however, the pro-opposition media's criticism of ZANU PF's politicians was more moderate in tone than the pro-government's criticism of opposition politicians.

Honesty is a third important characteristic for persons seeking political careers. Politicians whom the voters trust, who they perceive to be honest, and whom they do not suspect of having hidden agendas, always have an advantage over politicians whom the voters do not trust. In the struggle for political power, it is important both to build up one's own credibility, and to challenge that of one's opponents. Before the 2000 election, the media contributed more to the latter than to the former. As they saw it, the lack of honesty among politicians related primarily to two points: the contempt of the governing party for democratic rules and the opposition's hidden motives.

It was a recurring theme in the pro-opposition media that the ruling party would not hesitate to use dishonest means to win the election, a claim they supported with examples from previous elections. According to these media, voters should expect irregularities in connection with voter registration. Voters should also assume that constituency boundaries were drawn in such a way as to reduce opposition chances of winning seats. And last but not least, the most important reason for Mugabe's dislike of international observers was that their presence would reduce the opportunities for manipulating ballots and ballot boxes.

The pro-government media for their part voiced loud accusations that the opposition parties were concealing their true political motives. They were not seeking power in order to work for the benefit of Zimbabwe's black population, but to introduce neo-colonial rule in the interests of the country's white farmers and the British. Their message to the voters was clear: don't be taken in by the MDC's fair words, vote ZANU PF and avoid having the clock turned back to the pre-liberation situation. They also made the most of any opportunities to depict the MDC as a party that was scared of losing, and wanted to avoid a trial of strength with the Zimbabwean people, represented by ZANU PF. This point received special emphasis when the MDC for a short period hinted at the possibility of boycotting the election. By this means the pro-government media sought to show that the MDC was a party with no faith in its own chances if the people, rather than the party's foreign allies, were left to decide.

The media presentations show that relations between the main competitors in the election campaign were far from cordial, and that both the ruling party and its challengers had great difficulty in accepting each other's legitimacy, motives, and honesty. Political competition was a new experience for both parties, and it clearly emerged that it takes time to develop a democratic culture. To judge by the media coverage, however, there were clear differences between the approaches to the situation chosen by ZANU PF and the MDC. The criticism of the pro-oppositional newspaper was moderate in tone, and related to the ruling party's methods, not to its existence as a political alternative. The pro-government media were more heated in their comments on the opposition, and proclaimed very clearly that only ZANU PF as the trustees of the liberation heritage were worthy to rule the country. Only politicians with a background in the liberation struggle had a legitimate place in Zimbabwean politics, and any enemy of ZANU PF was an enemy of a free Zimbabwe.

MEDIATED DEMOCRACY

In countries where freedom of the press is not restricted, the media can adopt three main positions in their relationship to political parties and politicians (Bjørklund 1991). The first is to serve as loyal channels for particular parties and politicians, acting as reliable partners and enabling them to exercise a high degree of control over their political messages. Parties in such a position can feel sure that their political message will reach the voters and that their positions will be defended in the struggle for their favour. The second position is for the media to function as an independent arena, making broadcasting time and column space available to political actors of different shades of opinion. Neutral media of this kind place greater demands on the communicative skills of the politicians, in a political terrain in which none have protection against unfavourable comment and all are without permanent allies.

The third position arises when the media themselves function as political actors and plot their own political courses. Independent media of this kind introduce another type of actor into political life, and the politicians are obliged to relate to a wider range of political premises. In the period leading up to the 2000 election, both the ZBC and the newspapers within Zimpapers served as loyal outlets for Mugabe and ZANU PF. This role as a political channel was manifested in a number of ways. While all the state-controlled media gave great prominence to Mugabe's activities, as well as to ZANU PF's nomination process and other activities before the election, they contained very little on the MDC. Political events were constantly presented from a ZANU PF point of view, and in ways that brought out the party's advantages over its election rival. The MDC were given the precisely opposite treatment: on the rare occasions when they were mentioned, it was with few exceptions with a negative emphasis on their ability to solve the country's problems. In this way ZANU PF was free to carry on its political activities in the knowledge that the country's largest media would ensure that its policies were presented to the voters in a favourable light, and would refrain from calling attention to matters which the party preferred to keep out of the limelight.

All the pro-opposition newspapers adopted a strong negative attitude to the governing party and developed evident sympathy for the MDC. However, instead of serving as a channel for the MDC they behaved as independent actors, albeit with a definite political preference. They all made their political sympathies known by criticising the party they opposed rather than by promoting the one they favoured. They devoted much more space to criticising the governing party than to boosting the MDC, and this focus on ZANU PF left the MDC in the shadow. As a result, much of the support for the opposition was indirect. Although the pro-oppositional newspapers were eager to see ZANU PF replaced as the ruling party they did not give the MDC direct and unequivocally constructive support. Voters learned little about the substance of the MDC's policies or about the party's electioneering, and these newspapers did not market the MDC to anything like the same extent as the pro-governmental media did for ZANU PF.

It was in fact a conspicuous feature of the election campaign that the opposition parties did not make the most of the chances they had to challenge the vulnerability of the ruling party. As reflected in the media, the opposition's campaign showed two distinct characteristics. One was that it was defensive. In all essentials Mugabe and ZANU PF defined the terms and the contents of the campaign. Neither the MDC nor the pro-opposition newspapers managed to focus the debate on areas where they might have questioned ZANU PF's economic and social policies of recent years. Instead, issues that the Government wished to emphasise, and which distracted attention from some of the most urgent problems, dominated the agenda. A second feature of the opposition's election campaign is that it was negative. Both the MDC and the other opposition parties concentrated much more on what in their opinion was wrong with the government's policies than on what solutions they themselves had to offer to the same questions. This amounted to a failure by the opposition to acquaint the voters with its own policies. Running down other politicians is admittedly a well-tried strategy, but recent research has indicated that favourable media presentation of one's own party produces better results than criticism of one's opponents (Norris et al. 1999).

FUTURE PERSPECTIVES

Free media are a prerequisite for an open political discourse in society, and all former experience shows that access to the media is a decisive political resource in modern society. Parties and politicians who are not allowed to communicate through the media are under a considerable handicap compared to those who have as much media access as they want and on their own terms. By the end of the 1990s, ZANU PF had lost an important advantage over its political rivals in this respect. That this had a major impact in the run-up to the parliamentary election in 2000 is beyond doubt. As we have seen, the pro-opposition newspapers provided an important corrective to the pro-government media's one-sided support for ZANU PF.

Since then the conditions for freedom of expression have gradually worsened in Zimbabwe and the prospects for the future are bad.

During 2001 and the first half of 2002 president Mugabe tightened his grip on the country's media, both through new media laws and through the establishment of a Media and Information Commission, the task of which is to register and give accreditation to all media organizations and journalists. The restrictions on the activities of pro-opposition journalists imposed by the new laws have constituted a major setback for the freedom of the press and of expression in Zimbabwe.

The opposition's possibilities to make known its views were further reduced in September 2003 when The Daily News and its newly-established Sunday edition, The Daily News on Sunday, were closed down on the allegation of not having properly applied to get registered. The opposition has thus lost its most valuable mouthpiece, and to a large extent Mugabe's efforts to silence all media critical of ZANU PF have succeeded.

Thus, in the run-up to the 2005 parliamentary election president Mugabe had once again obtained a virtual information monopoly. The weekly media survey presented by the Media Monitoring Project Zimbabwe shows clearly the biased pro-ZANU PF points of view that the state-controlled media convey to their public. The 2005 election thus took place without a free and critical press and the opposition was almost invisible and without an outlet for making its policy known to the people. The election agenda was one-sided with a sole focus on issues favourable to the ZANU PF regime. This time no one was able to act as a watchdog, calling attention to unsolved problems, exposing reprehensible action on the part of the authorities, and ensuring that significant matters are not concealed from public view.

What Time is it in Political Journalism?

It was December 1994, Bill Clinton's first term, in the weeks after the spectacular Republican takeover in Congress. Adam Gopnik, writer for the New Yorker, sketched a portrait of the political press that I clipped because it drew on his many talents as a stylist. What he said may have been obvious to any alert and informed viewer, but it was also at odds with how journalists think of themselves and their problems. It remains that today. Remember, it was during the Clinton years that he wrote this:

> *"Any ordinary television viewer who has watched Presidential news conferences over the last couple of Administrations can't have failed to pick up a tone of high-minded moral indignation in the reporters' questions, which seem designed not so much to get at a particular fact or elicit a particular view as to dramatize the gulf in moral stature between the reporters and the President." ("Read All About It," the New Yorker, Dec. 12, 1994, not online.)*

Gopnik found a dearth of reasoning in the press think of the day, a vacuum where journalists might have developed stronger ideas. Since Watergate, he wrote:

> *the American press has undergone a transformation from an access culture to an aggression culture: the tradition, developed after the Civil War, in which a journalist's advancement depended on his intimacy with power, has mutated into one in which his success can also depend on a willingness to stage visible, ritualized displays of aggression. The reporter used to gain status by dining with his subjects; now he gains status by dining on them...*

The key word was displays. Gopnik looked with a drama critic's eye on the journalist's (increasingly televised) presentation of self. He told how the culture of aggression was fatally constrained in journalism; it could not develop into a new kind of political institution, for it "still has to thrive within the old institutions of the commercial press."

American newsrooms, he said, tend to suppress "political thought in the interests of an ideal (or at least the appearance) of objectivity." This produces strange results. Journalists now "relish aggression while still being prevented, by their own codes, from letting that aggression have any relation to serious political argument, let alone grown-up ideas about conduct and morality." I'll let him elaborate:

Aggression has become a kind of abstract form, practiced in a void of ideas, or even of ordinary sympathy. In a grim paradox, the media in America, because their aggression has been kept quarantined from good ideas, have become surprisingly vulnerable to bad ideas... the jaded tone and the prosecutorial tone are masks, switched quickly enough so that you can appear active and neutral at the same time. Or, to put it another way, the cynicism and the sanctimony turn out to be a little like electricity and magnetism - two aspects of a single field, perpetuating themselves in a thought-free vacuum.

Attempted use of the "gulf in moral stature" is still common. (I wrote about Wolf Blitzer doing it with Dennis Kucinich.) For example, Chris Matthews, the host of Hardball on MSNBC, was profiled this week in USA Today. He's been climbing in the ratings during the political season. On that count-440,000 viewers and gaining-Hardball is one of the few bright spots for the network. Listen to Matthews explain his success:

On Hardball, we assume that issues are important to the American people. What America does in the world, what kind of government we have, all that stuff is damn important... But we also know that politics, in addition to having incredibly high stakes, is not always on the level and that what politicians say about why they do things and what they say about interest groups and what they do to win votes is not the truth. You have to wangle that from them.

That's Matthews as truthteller, exposing those who are "not always on the level." Later in the same portrait, Mandy Grunwald appears. The former political consultant, now a peformer in what Eric Alterman and Michael Tomasky rightly call "journalism-related program activity," is a Chris Matthews admirer: "Chris doesn't put up with bull, which is the tough thing about doing his show. If people try to get away with just doing their talking points, he'll interrupt and say, 'That's ridiculous,' or, 'Come on, answer the question.'"

This is a rhetorical and visual stance, but also a favorite job description: the professional crap-detector, de-illusioned and well informed, sifting out the half truths, calling out the evasions, sizing up the scene in an analytical way, asking tough, necessary, cagey, impolite and just newsworthy questions. It's the self-image of choice for a great many who do political journalism today. It's what Tim Russert, Jody Wilgoren and Howard Fineman would probably say they're about. And it provides an easy answer to:

- Dear Journalist: who are you, politically speaking?
- Within politics, what kind of work do you do?
- And which side are you on, if not your own?

The consensus reply-the one most commonly repeated, readily defended, roundly believed in by journalists-is in serious trouble these days. It says:

Our politics? We're professionals who have no partisan role. We are neutral toward all parties, factions, candidates. We're on the public's side. We supply vital news, a context for understanding it, analysis and interpretation where needed. Beyond that we play the roles of crap-detector, truthteller, probing questioner of politicians and other players. Here, as everywhere, we are contrained by the journalist's imperatives of fairness, accuracy, relevance, timeliness, and equal treatment. And we try not to bore you. Those are our principles, those are our politics. Is that what you meant?

Well, no. It isn't. And that is why this belief system is in serious trouble. It answers a political question with an evacuation of politics, toward which professional correctness in journalism allows only neutrality and its endless equivalents- one of which is equal opportunity aggression in the watchdog role. Gopnik saw this attitude not as undesirable, but strangely non-descript.

For it fails to say anything meaningful about the journalist's role in the American political system as it stands. It is also relentlessly ahistorical, defeating thought about changes in public life that might present new problems or require new ideas. As the press scholar Michael Schudson once wrote, "The news media necessarily incorporate into their work a certain view of politics, and they will either do so intelligently and critically or unconsciously and routinely."

Leonard Downie, editor of the Washington Post, gave a speech last year at Harvard. Heard any of this before?

"So if you do tough investigative reporting about Democrats or about issues that are important to the left, you'll get a strong backlash from the left. Similarly, if you do tough investigative reporting of the Republicans or people on the right, you'll get a strong backlash from them. And I think this is also having an impact on the media. It's scaring people." (Quoted here.)

Reasoning like this is an example of what Gopnik meant by a vacuum. There is no attempt by Downie to examine and understand either backlash. The noise around him is just the predictable squealing when the press does its job. What's the job? Apolitical truthteller; and (shrug) some don't like it. (See my earlier post about Downie's press think.)

Here the ritual of balance cancels out the criticism from both wings and locates journalism where it should be, and must remain: between left and right, telling inconvenient truths to both, and resented for that reason. (What other reason could there be?) The imagery-press in the middle against the extremes-is a case of what Gopnik called "abstract form" in journalistic argument, where practices are defended "in a void of ideas, or even of ordinary sympathy."

The excruciating post-Scream interview that Howard Dean felt he had to submit to, with his wife beside him, meant watching Diane Sawyer of ABC News "relish" a certain style of aggression lacking in "grown-up ideas about conduct and morality," to quote Gopnik again. It's true that Sawyer is a celebrity journalist, and not at all typical of the larger- tribe. But his point was that Sawyer and other journalists on television think with the ideas of the tribe- and give evidence of the same vacuum by being, uh, vacuous.

The big, consensus stories at the time of Dean's sit down with Sawyer were the scream in Iowa and the "temper, temper" issue, along with "where's the wife?" Both were proxies for "is Dean presidential enough?" and "is he a normal American?" The herd mind of the campaign press had struck; these were the "issues" for Dean. And Sawyer conducted an interview that stuck entirely to that script- refusing in bald fashion to think for herself. So stylized were the results that she had to ask at one point:

> *One thing I actually heard somebody say is, this is like Bill and Hillary Clinton. This is the stand by your man interview. The public relations event. Does it feel like that?*

That is questioning that has left politics-and all the concerns of politics-behind, even as it enters into the game and affects it. Gopnik had warned about such. Ten years later, the press is still officially attached to, "We're professionals who have no partisan role- end of story." But the costs of denial and of reasoning in a vacuum have built up over the years. There are stresses and fractures that can no longer be ignored. Default reasoning in journalism seems more and more unreasoning about what's going on out there. Here, then, is a tour of recent commentary that tries to tell what time it is in the American press- politically speaking.

Howard Kurtz: Drop bad habits. "It's time for political reporters to swear off some long-standing habits," wrote Howard Kurtz on Monday. The habits worth dropping were over-reliance on the money chase, polls, endorsements and ground organization in judging a candidate's strength. They all performed poorly in predicting the 2004 race. That, of course, is another habit that could be dropped- "a prediction-obsessed culture in which many pundits and journalists were all but writing off candidates as the voting began and constantly trying to push the narrative to the next phase."

In a downcast mood, Mark Halperin, ABC's political director, told Kurtz: "Any political reporter whose humility level has not at least quintupled based on the events of this cycle should probably find something else to do in four years." What he means by humility is realizing: we did many stories, we knew very little about what was going on. That's a discouraging result. Kurtz's ideas for fixing it are mild, but if the bad habits he names were dropped, there would room for lively argument over what should replace them. And this would require of the press its best political thought.

Tim Porter: Time to get off the defensive. At First Draft, ex-newspaper editor Tim Porter is saying: re-gain your nerve, journalists of America. Writing about this provocative column from Eric Alterman and Michael Tomasky, Porter says now is the time to:

invigorate a profession that has allowed itself to be cowed into political correctness of all varieties-left, right and center-by a frameset of meta-messages that taint journalists as liberal pawns, conservative dupes or middle-of-the-road wimps. Taunted and attacked into stagnation, and therefore bereft of the serious purpose for which it, and it alone of all professions, is granted constitutional protection, journalism fills the void with faux news.

"It's time to start talking about what's good about journalism and what can be done to make it better," Porter writes. " It's time to get off defense and take the offensive. It's time, as Alterman and Tomasky put it, for the 'ambitious men and women of the Fourth Estate to reassert their power and professional pride.'" The end to stagnation will come when people in the press reclaim their power and re-examine their purpose. How else to get there, but through political argument that overcomes the taunting?

Geneva Overholser: Let's talk about Fox. Overholser, in her Poynter column, has another "it's time to..." The doctrine of objectivity, she says, has been successfully challenged by Fox News Channel. Let's stop pretending. It's time to have the conversation:

Fox News is arguably the first mainstream, widely distributed news medium to leave the objectivity God behind. And it looks as if it will be far from the last. A group calling itself "Progress Media," for example, is now aiming to form a liberal radio network, and Al Gore is pursuing a liberal cable TV network.

If we're jettisoning the objectivity commandment, though, shouldn't we have the discussion? You can make a strong case for it, you can make a strong case against it, but you can't make any case at all until you acknowledge that it's happening.

Overholser is saying: we don't have one model of political journalism any more, there's two. Our long history with a partisan press is being revived by Fox, and there will be others. (She resigned from the National Press Foundation board when it gave an award to Fox News anchor Brit Hume.) Let the case be made for the revival of partisan rules in journalism. Let the gods of objectivity restate their case against. Any way you look at it, this is a political argument the press needs to have- about itself.

Jim Bettinger: We're too much the establishment. Bettinger, a newspaper journalist for twenty years, is director of the Knight Fellows program at Stanford University. Writing in the new Nieman Reports about the recall election in California ("The Anger Journalists Never Fully Understood," Winter 2003) he says:

> *Now journalists face the challenge of having an awful lot to learn about what happened, with perhaps not much time to learn what they need to know. This challenge arises not because the coverage of the recall was bad. It wasn't. In fact, by measures that serious journalists use to evaluate political coverage, it was very good. But good coverage didn't seem to matter much and, in fact, it served to link journalists to an established political order that voters were determined to chase out of office three years ahead of schedule.*

To Bettinger, it's past time to admit that "journalists are entwined in established politics." The recall election won by Arnold Schwarzenegger "showed this graphically and also demonstrated how angry a significant segment of voters are at that established political order." But he has more to say, words many conservative critics say they rarely hear from figures in the mainstream press:

The fact remains that a significant segment of the public believes- to a moral certainty-that mainstream media work from an agenda of actively promoting liberal political goals and that they work in tandem with the traditional political system.

As journalists, we need to figure out ways to connect with these angry voters and disentangle ourselves from the political establishment, rather than dismiss this new political force as crazies who just aren't like us

Bettinger thinks this "disentangling"-certainly a political project in journalism-is an urgent matter. The ground is shifting beneath the press. Reaching the disillusioned with a new argument is going to be hard, but the risk of not trying is greater:

The warning I take away from the recall election's coverage is that serious journalism risks becoming irrelevant to a political process that may be undergoing fundamental change. For those of us who want to see journalism be a major force in democratic society and not just a constitutionally protected license to make money, significant challenges lie ahead. The toughest one: figuring out how to reach growing numbers of disillusioned citizens without pandering to them or jettisoning our core values.

Alterman and Tomasky: Rouse yourself, press, you have the power. Writing in the American Prospect, Eric Alterman and Michael Tomasky also sense some movement. But their eyes are on the state of power politics between the White House and the Washington press, and the degree to which journalists can be a true oppositional force. "Are our national media-schoolyard silly during campaign 2000, by turns somnolent and sycophantic ever since-starting to rouse themselves from their long torpor?"

In the course of giving five recommendations for spine-stiffening, Alterman and Tomasky note the no-access terms the press has been handed by the Bush White House. "On a regular basis, our greatest media institutions are accepting conditions that every undergraduate journalism student in the country is taught to reject," they write. "Individual reporters, scrambling for access and scoops, can't change this on their own. It's up to their bosses and owners." And the bosses and owners have a lot of power, with which they can back up their journalists:

What's one presidential administration to them? In time, Bush will be back in Crawford swatting Titleists. The Sulzbergers and the Grahams, to say nothing of General Electric and AOL Time Warner, will never be removed from office. That their journalists in Washington-with a small but still significant number of admirable exceptions-have quietly caved in to these conditions may or may not be unethical, but it is disgraceful. That the owners have let it happen will be their shameful legacy.

Alterman and Tomasky treat the press as a player in a contest for power in official Washington. The press should understand its underlying might and use it against truth management by the White House.

Dan Walters: Arnold is coming into our house now. Walters has been The Sacramento Bee's political columnist since 1984. He agreed that the serious press had been successfully bypassed by Schwarzenegger during the recall. But as governing in Sacramento begins, "those of us in the real political media will also have our shot, because the nuts and bolts of governance are far more complicated and treacherous than selling a simplistic campaign message."

Journalists who covered the recall "tended to be pure political reporters who specialize in campaigns-and often know little about, and usually ignore, the intricacies of government as they obsess on polls, television ads, and other forms of political minutiae." Listen to what's in store for the new Governor:

But once Schwarzenegger takes office, he will face the Capitol's resident press corps, some of whose members have been tracking legislation and administrative policy for decades, and he will have a much more difficult time blowing smoke on the budget and other issues.

In the blunt account that Walters gives, the political press has already proven its potency by sinking the previous Governor:

Gray Davis could tell him about that. After all, it was the Capitol press corps' intense and critical news coverage of his actions as governor that sent Davis's approval ratings on a tailspin from 60- plus percent to just over 20 percent and set the stage for the Schwarzenegger phenomenon. He's coming into our domain now, and we won't tolerate campaign-style sloganeering as a substitute for substantive action on the budget and other critical issues.

Jim Bettinger, in response to a question I asked him, emails with this:

> *"I think there are some parallels between the Howard Dean campaign coverage and the California recall coverage, particularly in the difficulty that main-stream journalists had in grasping the energy of the Dean wave. This is not surprising. The radar of mainstream political journalism is aimed pretty high and calibrated for large objects, and a swarm of small objects flying close to the ground will go largely undetected.*
>
> *"This was true of the recall and true of Dean. The difference is that national political journalists had a lot longer to examine the Dean phenomenon after it got on the radar screen than did the California political journalists, and they didn't have the dominating presence of Schwarzenegger to contend with."*

Political philospher and weblogger Peter Levine comments on this post:

> *Along similar lines, I've been asking myself, "What would happen if reporters showed more respect for our democratic institutions?" There's a big debate about whether reporters are too solicitous, or too critical, of various major figures, especially the President of the United States. But that's not what I mean. In fact, to respect democratic institutions might mean paying less attention to individuals and their motives and fortunes.*

For example, who cares whether George W. Bush supports the anti-gay-marriage amendment in order to appease his conservative base, as the Times explains in its front page "news analysis" today? (By the way, we can't know his motives, and the only people who possibly have insight are Administration insiders, who aren't trustworthy sources.)

Imagine, instead, that the Times explained that a struggle between majoritarian institutions and courts has arisen because the fourteenth amendment requires "equal protection under the law," yet many voters see marriage as a sacrament that can only apply to heterosexual couples.

Citizens need to wrestle with what the fourteenth amendment means and how it can coexist with one-person, one-vote. Respectful coverage might demonstrate that this is not an easy issue-not for those of us who strongly favor gay marriage but also believe in democracy; not for those who oppose gay marriage but also believe in equality.

Hence those decision-makers in Washington are not just playing games for political advantage. They are in a tough spot morally and they are doing their jobs.

2

POLITICAL JOURNALISM AND EUROPEANIZATION

The paper's central focus is on how journalism, including reporting and commentating, has responded to the perceived changes in the political environment that result from advancing European integration. It provides general answers on the press' contribution to the Europeanisation of political information. First, a contents analysis informs about newspapers' European coverage.

Then, we examine journalists' perceptions, of their own performances, potential sources and readers, news production, journalistic practices and organisational aspects, from interview data. A key question is whether covering European affairs is similar or different to national politics, and whether journalists adopt a more passive 'neutral' informative educative role, or see Europe as an opportunity for a more 'active' political role. The empirical data source is cross-nationally comparative covering seven countries (UK, F, D, NL, I, ESP, CH) based on contents analysis of four newspapers per country, and interviews with more than 100 journalists. Our main findings are that, with the exception of The Sun in Britain, there is little evidence for the press as a source of Euroscepticism, and covering Europe is really 'business as usual'. Most newspapers print pro-European positions. Journalists' advocacy over Europe is primarily intended to inform and educate the public by raising awareness. We find little evidence for journalists acting overtly as political actors.-

INTRODUCTION

The press' role and performance in covering European politics is commonly criticized as contributing to the European Union's perceived 'democratic deficit', its lack of visibility, resonance and legitimacy in the 'hearts and minds' of citizens. In addition, politicians seldom miss an opportunity to blame the press for not delivering the 'correct message', especially when they fail in their European integration objectives, such as the French and Dutch 2005 Constitution referendums. Likewise, British governments regularly blame the press for the salience of Euroscepticism which they see as a significant brake on the UK's participation in the EU. In this chapter, we direct attention at the intentions and efforts by journalists to shape the coverage of European affairs.

For Schlesinger (1999:276/7), the emergence of a 'European sphere of publics' requires the dissemination of a European news agenda, that becomes part of the every-day news-consuming habits of European audiences, and entails that publics come to understand citizenship and belonging as at least in part transcending the nation-state. Clearly, the supply of political information by the press is crucial in determining the possibility of any moves toward such a situation.

The press acts both as a messenger who selects and reports on significant political events, and as a commentator, a political actor who advances specific opinions in the public sphere. Our central focus is on how journalism, including both reporting and commentating, has responded to the perceived changes in the political environment that result from advancing European integration. Instead of blaming the media with a call to 'shoot the messenger', we address the media's performance over European politics as an open research question that requires empirical investigation. If there are deficits in the media's performance, they need to be understood and explained within context of the relationship between media and political systems (Hallin and Mancini 2004) and the multi-levelling of politics.

We aim to provide general answers on the press' contribution to the Europeanisation of political information. Specifically, we examine the factors which drive the level and form of coverage of European affairs. First, our contents analysis informs about newspapers' European coverage. Then, we examine journalists' perceptions of different aspects of the political communication process over Europe, evaluating their own performances, their perceptions of potential sources and readers, news production, journalistic practices and organisational aspects. We attempt to establish whether covering European affairs is similar or different to national politics, and how journalists envisage their own roles, in particular, whether they adopt a more passive 'neutral' informative-educative role, or whether they see Europe as an opportunity for a more 'active' political role.

Such aspects may vary, cross-nationally, across newspaper type, or across different specialists and practices within journalism. Thus we adopt a comparative approach that covers seven countries, different types of daily newspapers, and different types of journalists. Our primary focus is on the press within nation-states, which given linguistic, cultural and commercial obstacles, is the most likely candidate for a 'European sphere of publics' compared to a European transnational mass media (Schlesinger 1999). Nonetheless, we include four examples of the small elite-oriented 'transnational press' to add an extra comparative dimension.

We now review research on journalism and Europe and outline a conceptual model for studying the media's 'dual role' as an institutionalised forum for political debate and as a political actor who advances its own positions in the public sphere. We then provide details on our comparative research design and methods. This approach structures the subsequent empirical analyses of news contents and journalists' perceptions. Finally, we relate our central findings to existing debates. Conceptualising the Media's 'Dual Role' and Factors Shaping Coverage Research on the press and European affairs is an emergent, fragmented and underdeveloped field. There are a few studies on aspects of news production and journalism, evaluating EU correspondents on national papers (Morgan 1995, Baisnée 2002), and on the EU's communication performance (Meyer 1999, Tumber 1995). There are also some studies which combine contents analysis with interviews, applying cross-national comparison, though often -understandably given limited resources- restricted to specific issue events or short time-scales (de Vreese 2001; Gleissner and De Vreese 2005; Trenz 2005).

Despite such advances, there is relatively little in the way of 'joined up' approaches, addressing both contents and news production processes, systematically and cross-nationally, at a general level. Donsbach and Patterson (2004:253) note this is generally a problem in communication studies on political journalism, 'Explanatory comparative analyses...are virtually nonexistent, even though the field is of high scientific interest.' Whereas Hallin and Mancini (2004:2) point out the resultant pitfalls: 'Most of the literature on the média is highly ethnocentric, in the sense that it refers only to the experience of a single country, yet is written in general terms, as though the model that prevailed in that country were universal.' Noting such caveats, it is still possible to summarise that existing research emphasizes press' characteristics that purportedly act as barriers to, or at least slow down, the emergence of 'Europeanized' news.

These include: journalists' applying 'national' frameworks of interpretation, missing 'new' and different qualities of Europeanised politics; poor linkages of news gathering and production to EU institutions; journalists' poor language skills and knowledge deficits; remoteness of Brussels from domestic news rooms and editors' decisions; European politics' obscurity and lack of 'news values'; (Morgan 1995, Baisnée 2002); and newspaper organisation's and their proprietor's supposed Eurosceptic political agendas (Anderson and Weymouth 1999).

Given the relative absence of systematic empirical evidence, however, much remains informed speculation. According to de Vreese (2001: 283), 'Further research should address the nature of media attention to EU affairs during routine periods that are not dominated by key events as well as investigate systematically the role of the EU in domestic political and economic news.' Moving in this direction, for our purposes of large-scale cross-national comparison it was necessary to develop a general model to examine the role of the press.

For this project, journalists in media organisations are conceived as fulfilling a 'dual function' (Koopmans and Statham 2002; Koopmans and Pfetsch 2003). First, they are seen as mediators of political information from external sources. Here their actions shape the information flows that are of crucial importance to polities -national, supranational and regional- which rely on a free flow of information as the basis of democratic legitimisation, responsiveness, accountability and participation (Koopmans and Erbe 2004, Statham and Gray 2005). Secondly, journalists are actors in their own right, who contribute to processes of opinion-formation by commentating on political affairs.

To arrive at these 'outputs' of political information, it is first necessary to examine 'inputs', and the actor-relationships which produce them, both internal and external to the news production process.

Combining these positions produces an integrated general model that importantly allows us to examine different aspects of the process, and their influence relative to one another. Although this general approach requires a simplification of specific aspects of the political communication process that receive more a comprehensive and detailed scrutiny elsewhere, we justify this parsimony by the significant gains of an account that positions journalism within the overall process of political communication.

Here our topical focus is the European news. Stated simply, what drives European coverage?

READERSHIP'S DEMAND

A first relationship runs from the public to the media organisation. Publics interact with political information as a consumption process that can lead to opinion formation. Newspapers relate to readerships, both as a market of consumers, and as an audience and public constituency with whom it shares a cultural milieu of specific political values. Also newspapers are commercial enterprises that need to advance their market share relative to competitors, and establish loyalty among a readership who identify with the newspaper and buy it regularly. Indeed, Schlesinger (1999: 277) considers this market-seeking behaviour much more the driving force for media responses to Europeanisation than the search for a new public imagined in normative theory.

In this competitive marketplace, it could be that newspapers respond to perceptions of readership's demand

(1) for political information. The level and type of readership demand is likely to be a condition that influences coverage, because newspapers have incentives to appeal to the political tastes and understandings of their readers. For example, if public interest in European affairs is low, there are fewer incentives for newspapers to report them. If the public views European politics as a sub-issue of national politics, coverage is likely to try and meet readership expectations by promoting national interpretative frameworks, rather than multi-levelled, EUsupranational, or Europeanised ones. If the political institutions of the European Union come to be seen by its citizens as important to their lives, this would raise readerships' demand for information, and increase incentives for newspapers to cover European affairs. General changes in public understandings of the political world tend to be slow and lag behind institutional developments, in this case advancing European integration. Perhaps most effective in raising public interest and awareness and demand for information are key events, such as the introduction of the Euro, or responses to BSE, which affect people's everyday lives and demonstrate the European Union's political power and relevance. Overall, the level and type of readership demand remains a limiting condition that influences the media's decision-making over coverage.

COLLECTIVE ACTORS' AGENDA-BUILDING

A second important relationship runs from collective actors to media organisations. Newspapers depend to a large extent on 'inputs' of information from the political discourse which is produced by collective actors from political institutions, social and economic interest groups, and NGOs, making claims over events. In this view, the public sphere carried by the media is a competitive field of political discourse where collective actors engage in acts of 'strategic political communication' (Kriesi 2004) to make their demands visible to a wider audience, in the attempt to exert political influence. Given the limited carrying capacity of the media, collective actors try to influence each other by mobilising publicly visible information, demands, and arguments that compete for attention. In the literature, such attempts are referred to as 'agenda-building' or 'agenda-setting' (Hilgartner and Bosk 1988, Lang and Lang 1983, McCombs and Shaw 1972, Everett and Dearing 1986).

For collective actors, public visibility is crucial because it allows a message access to wider publics. This gives it the potential for 'agenda-building' by resonating with the opinions of allies and opponents, and the public, in the attempt to gain legitimacy, as the most credible, reasonable and authoritative version of political reality. We distinguish two types of agenda-building activities. First, collective actors mobilise public campaigns (2a) in relation to political events (Kriesi 2004), sometimes explicitly staging 'pseudo' events to attract attention, and increase their chances of selection by journalists. Second, collective actors engage in 'source strategies' (Schlesinger and Tumber 1994, Anderson 1991) (2b).

These are purposeful attempts to target and 'symbolically package' (Gamson and Modigliani 1989) political information directly at journalists in order to shape coverage in a way that privileges specific opinions and interpretations of events. This distinction is really a continuum, with 'campaigns' targeting journalists indirectly through the construction of events which carry information, and 'source strategies' directly through the mobilisation of information. Successful 'agenda-building' by collective actors influences the resources of political discourse and events that are available to journalists for selecting, reporting and commenting on. However, some collective actors have more resources to engage in agenda-building than others. Political institutional actors have routine channels of access to the news agenda through their publicity activities, such as press releases, which cross the threshold of public significance relatively easily, because their actions have important public consequences. Less powerful actors, such as protest groups, usually do not possess routine channels of access to the news agenda, and have to invest more efforts to make their claims appear publicly significant. As a consequence powerful institutional 'voices' tend to be more present in media discourse than those of civil society actors and social movements (Schlesinger and Tumber 1994).

With regard to European news coverage, the supply of available political information will depend on who makes claims about Europe, and how they mobilise and frame them. If actors representing national political institutions make more agenda-building efforts over Europe than European ones, their specific 'national' agenda of political claims will importantly shape the contents of the information resource-pool facing journalists. Conversely, if the European institutions do not attempt to advance their positions publicly, they will simply not be heard by journalists, and have fewer chances of reaching the news compared to actors who do. Meyer (1999) cites the EU's lack of a co-ordinated communications strategy as contributing to a 'deficit' of information for citizens.

Generally one would expect institutional actors with their greater resources than civil society actors for agenda-building, to importantly shape the available contents of political discourse. However, given the advancing multi-levelling of political actors' relationships, it could be that there are new opportunities for civil society actors to mobilise claims over Europe, when compared to the established setting of national politics. It also needs underlining that collective actors with different scopes and types have vested interests in shaping how political discourse represents European affairs.

For example, national political actors will advance their own position relative to European institutions by promoting a political discourse where European affairs is viewed within an interpretative framework of 'national interests'. In addition, national governments sometimes seek to shift the blame for perceived problems 'up' onto the supranational level (Imig and Tarrow 2001). European institutions need to make themselves heard to counteract such tendencies.

The general point, which appears self-evident but is sometimes overlooked, is that journalists can only make their decisions over selection, reporting and commentating on public affairs, in relation to the political discourse that is visible to them (Koopmans and Pfetsch 2003). Thus the political discourse over Europe which results from competing actors' agenda-building is a crucial factor that limits and shapes journalists' decisions over coverage. The important point, is that any perceived or real 'deficit' in the public visibility of European affairs, is not necessarily -as is often claimed- due to the media's poor performance, but could, and arguably is more likely to, result from inadequacies in the performance of the political system, and the inability of political institutions and collective actors to present important problems to the public, thereby allowing wider deliberation processes.

NEWSPAPERS' ORGANISATIONAL CULTURE (EDITORIAL LINE)

News organisations operate within constraints and opportunities shaped by commercial and institutional factors, including ownership, market share, and a context defined by the specific relationship between the media and political system (Hallin and Mancini 2004, Blumler and Gurevitch 1995). Here we take these macrocontextual factors largely for granted and focus on the media organisation as an environment which provides specific constraints and incentives for journalists. Journalists are people who take decisions directly affecting news contents (Donsbach and Patterson 2004). This definition-covers editors and reporters, who participate in daily decisions that influence the gathering and selection processes for information, as well as interpreting and actually writing stories and commentaries that become 'news'. Journalists are professionals too.

They belong to a social group sharing a common orientation and ethos that affects how they see their work (Weaver 2005; Tumber and Prentoulis 2005). According to McQuail (1994: 198), for journalists '(t)he height of professional skill is the exercise of a practical craft, which delivers the required institutional product, characterized by a high degree of objectivity, key marks of which are obsessive facticity and neutrality of attitude.' However, within professional journalism, there is variation between different news organisations and newspaper types, and across different press cultures or national 'models' (Mancini 2005), in how journalists' perceive their roles.

A first 'internal' factor to news production which shapes coverage is that journalists write on behalf of news organisations with an established institutional culture and editorial line for representing politics and advancing opinions. Newspapers usually have a clear relationship to institutional politics, and position themselves with an identity on the left or right of, or independently from, party politics.

This collective identity derives from the position of a newspaper in the national media landscape which is based on the relationship between the media and political systems (Mazzoleni 1992, Hallin and Mancini 2004). In addition, newspapers address readerships with specific characteristics, for example, as broadsheets for educated elites, or as tabloids for mass general publics. The specific organisational culture (3) of a newspaper is a shared collective identity that finds expression in its 'editorial line'.

Journalists work within this 'organisational culture', and their autonomy as individuals is relatively limited to writing within the established line, style, formats and genre of their newspaper. In general, most journalists see themselves as professionals who write on behalf of their newspaper and consciously identify with its 'editorial line'. Seen as an internalised set of values, this factor shapes journalists' decisions and thereby influences coverage, sometimes in direct and obvious ways. For example, journalists on newspapers closely linked with political parties, such as L'Humanité which is linked to the French Communist party, are more likely to report events in which this party is involved.

This also impacts on the coverage of European affairs. For example, L'Humanité's European coverage is likely to be influenced by Communist Party's level of activism over Europe, and it is likely to portray European affairs in a way that fits the Communist Party's Euroscepticism.

JOURNALISTS' INFORMATION GATHERING

Another factor which influences news production is the gathering of political information by journalists. In general, the scope, capacity and resource base of the infrastructure of an organisation affects the flow and type of political information that is available as a potential resource for journalists. For example, a newspaper with a specialist correspondent based in Brussels is likely to receive better quality information on events in supranational European politics, than one that relies on a domestic reporter, or on news agencies. The newsgathering infrastructure of a newspaper is likely to depend on organisational factors such as available resources, the 'editorial line', and the need to provide information for a specific readership. Within this organisational context, journalists also mobilise-their own resources, networks and supply-lines for gathering information. Journalists sometimes gather information at their own initiative through investigative journalism (4a) about public affairs, and also through their established source-relationships (4b). Such news gathering efforts and the 'selection' of information which it brings, compared to possible alternatives, is a factor that can influence coverage.

First, the extent to which journalists actively set out to investigate and gather information on European affairs, is likely to depend on whether they perceive existing sources of political information provided by collective actors' agenda-building to be adequate.

Thus, if journalists perceive deficits in the public visibility of or information provision by political institutions, such as the European Commission, they may consider it a public duty to collect information that allows them the opportunity to report and comment on such affairs. Second, journalists' relationships with their established sources can influence how they report on European affairs.

For example, if journalists' established relationships with sources are with national political actors rather than European ones, it could be that when covering Europe they continue to use these sources rather than look for new ones. This would be likely to privilege the representation of national rather than supranational viewpoints on European affairs, as a direct result of journalistic news-gathering practices.

Alternatively, journalists could see European integration as a topic that is inadequately supplied by their source-relationships, and seek out, and be receptive to, information from new sources. In this case, journalists' newsgathering practices open up opportunities to new actors as potential sources.

JOURNALISTS' SELECTION OF NEWS

Journalists' decisions on how to represent public events and express opinions on behalf of the newspaper are clearly important factors that shape the specific constructions of political reality that appear as 'outputs'. Here, we focus on news selection (5) as an aspect of journalists' practices that potentially influences coverage. When reporting and commentating, journalists make decisions to select which of the many public events and claims-making acts are 'newsworthy'. This selection process is crucial to the resultant 'outputs'. First, the media's limited carrying capacity necessitates choices about the public significance of competing events and claimsmaking. And second, journalists tend to impose a 'media logic' (Mazzoleni 1992) in their selection decisions which preferences the chances of specific types of events and actors appearing.

In general, journalists' selections of political events for coverage will be drawn from their perceptions of the political discourse and made from the perspective of their newspaper's organisational culture and editorial line. Although this salience in the political discourse shifts the media's attention onto specific events and issues which they must follow to maintain their reputation and standing as newspapers of public record, Galtung and Ruge's classic research (1965), identified that journalists also apply their own specific criteria of 'news values' to determine 'newsworthiness'. In this view, journalists' practices are considered a process of successive selections, and their perceptions of 'newsworthiness' a complex set of criteria where the characteristics of an event -prominence, human interest, conflict, 'the unusual', timeliness, cultural proximity (Shoemaker and Reese 1996)- can influence its likelihood of being selected. Thus the media's own 'logic' can potentially influence the selection and coverage of public affairs. For example, events with a high level of drama or conflict, or claims by important public figures and personalities have high 'news values', which is why collective actors often stage protest events with such qualities. If events related to European affairs do not fit the established 'media logic', for example, if journalists' 'news values' demand exciting conflicts between personalities and European affairs tend to be technocratic debates between faceless bureaucrats, they are less likely to be reported or the subject of editorial commentary.

MEDIA'S AGENDA-SETTING AND ADVOCACY

Another important factor which potentially shapes 'outputs', is the extent to which journalists attempt to promote their own stances, and in which ideological direction they do so, when writing for a newspaper. When reporting, journalists act as 'mediators' who produce a representation of the 'external' political discourse constructed by collective actors' claims-making acts in relation to events. When commentating, journalists are claims-makers who advance opinions and evaluations in the political discourse. This dual function is clearly expressed in the structure of newspapers, which have distinct sections for news reports on public affairs, and editorials advancing the newspaper's position. However, there is a degree of overlap, in that some newspapers allow scope for commentating within news reports, and editorials are usually selected and written in response to 'external' political events. Also, roles vary within the organisation: editors, leader writers and commentators have more say over what events to select and how to portray them than beat reporters.

Operating within their newspaper's organisational culture, journalists have opportunities for moving beyond 'neutral' or 'objective' factual coverage of events and taking up an 'advocate' (Janowitz 1975) or politically 'partisan' stance (Donsbach and Patterson 2004). They may actively attempt to promote opinionformation processes among their readerships by the way they construct political reality. Such acts of advocacy are contained in the contents of 'outputs': media representations of claims-making over political events; and the media's own claimsmaking. These are the journalists' own 'agenda-setting' (McCombs and Shaw 1972) efforts to influence public deliberation and opinion formation, as well as collective actors and political institutions, and appear as a 'feedback loops' from their 'outputs'.

First, coverage that represents the political discourse requires placing events and opinions within a context, which is likely to privilege specific actors and opinions, over others. Such effects have been called 'second-level agenda-setting' (6a) Eilders and Voltmer 2003) and are often referred to in discussions of the media's 'bias' and 'framing' when representing public affairs.

Second, the media's own claims-making or advocacy (6b) is a direct attempt at agenda-setting and framing the political discourse over public affairs. Here journalists focus public attention on issues and make attempts to influence the way they are politically understood, which may lead to opinion formation, consensus and dissent building, and possibly collective mobilisation. Such efforts are discussed in literature on the media's political influence, including its role as a 'political actor' (Page 1996), 'advocacy', and 'media framing' (Iyengar 1993). However, it is necessary to elaborate on the possible dimensions of 'advocacy'.

News coverage may be informative-educative, and attempt to raise public awareness and knowledge about a perceived problem, or it may be partisan and advance a specific ideological stance in the attempt to build a constituency of supporters. These dimensions are not mutually exclusive: the 'informative-educative' attempts to promote an issue though raising awareness; whereas the 'partisan', attempts to intentionally attribute it with a specific ideological 'bias'.

Another variable dimension is the autonomy of journalists to engage in advocacy, which can be measured by the extent to which journalists' claims-making efforts over an issue vary from the political line of the newspaper's established organisational culture. Europe may be an issue over the media engages in advocacy.

For example, given that ideological cleavages over Europe largely cross-cut left-right cleavages, the resultant lack of clear cues from political actors, could impact on whether journalists adopt an advocacy role. It could affect the extent to which they engage in advocacy over Europe, the ideological position they take, and their autonomy. First, the media's advocacy could be informative-educative but not ideologically partisan. Here its coverage would raise public understandings of perceived problems but without taking a partisan Eurosceptic or pro-European stance, for example, by blaming the ineffectiveness of either European or national politicians to address concerns adequately.

Alternatively, advocacy over Europe may be less than one might expect for an important topic, for example, if journalists decide to mobilise opinion only on issues where they receive clear cues from their allies in the political system. Third, journalists could see European affairs as an opportunity to push their own agenda, and advance a 'partisan' political stance, underlining their autonomy from those positions expressed in the political system. This pro- or anti-European stance could be independent, or follow that of a specific political party or faction. Newspapers could even institutionalise this role by running their own pro-European or Eurosceptic campaigns and making Europe a key element of their 'editorial line'. Much depends on journalists' perceptions of their role relative to the political system, which may vary across newspaper or journalist type, or national setting.

Research Design: Cross-national, Cross-newspaper, Cross-journalist Others emphasise television (de Vreese 2001), but our study takes newspapers as a mass medium of public record that allows a higher level of discursive elaboration over political events. Newspapers also allow for a clearer distinction between the reporting (reports) and commentating (editorials) functions. We cover seven countries, undertaking a contents analysis of 32 newspapers, and detailed structured interviews with 110 journalists. This makes ours one of the most extensive comparative studies of journalism.

It was not logistically feasible to cover all newspapers. We selected four newspapers per country which together were seen as 'best fit' functional equivalents for 'representing' their national media landscape. Our selection criteria also required variation by four types of newspaper per country (left-broadsheet, right-broadsheet, tabloid or popular, regional) and four types of journalist per newspaper (Editor/ lead writer, EU correspondent, journalist covering agriculture, journalist covering immigration). Overall, this research strategy allows the flexibility to compare across countries, newspaper types, and journalist types.

We selected two broadsheets considered newspapers of public record with nationwide distribution, varied by political affiliation (centre-left v. centre-right). This allowed investigation of a possible 'left-right' cleavage by newspapers over Europe. We added a mass circulation popular or tabloid newspaper, to allow for investigation of variation by whether a newspaper addressed elite (broadsheet) or general (tabloid/

popular) publics, given that Europe tends to be an elite issue. Last, we took a regional newspaper, to examine variations between national and sub-national media, in the light of the special emphasis that Europe has given to regions and their cultures. Our selection of journalist types was governed by three requirements, to be able to: vary across different professional roles within the media organisation; distinguish between journalists who 'report' on political events, and those who 'commentate'; and distinguish between journalists who are EU specialists and those who working on 'normal' beats (immigration and agriculture) where Europe is sometimes and sometimes not relevant.

Finding cross-national functional equivalents among newspapers is not straightforward, largely due to the nature of the subject matter. As the seminal research by Hallin and Mancini (2004) demonstrates, cross-national variations in newsprint landscapes are to a large extent shaped by, and constitutive of, differences in the political systems of those countries.

Specific media systems, their media landscapes and press cultures, are products of, derived from, and constitutive of specific types of liberal democracies, and reflect their important political cleavages. For this reason, it is not adequate simply to fill the cells constituting our four 'ideal' functional equivalents for newspapers, but selection needed to allow for additional variation in specific countries, to more accurately represent the key political cleavages, which are also reflected in their newsprint landscapes.

Our final newspaper selection was taken in consultation with national experts. Selection of centre-left and centre-right broadsheets was relatively straightforward. Although countries with federal political systems and/or important regionalist governments, such as Germany and Italy, have newspapers originating from specific regions, some of these can be considered to address national readerships.

Thus Süddeūtsche Zeitung and Frankfurter Allgemeine Zeitung have their regional origins expressed in their titles, and retain a limited regional bias, as does the Milan-centred Corriere della Sera, but they can be broadly considered as newspapers of national record. Selection of regional newspapers was also relatively unproblematic. Here we took newspaper which covered a sizeable region, with a distinct political, cultural and/or linguistic heritage.

For example, in Spain, we selected La Vanguardia which serves Catalonia, the Scotsman for Scotland in the UK, and a newspaper from the east, the Leipziger Allgemeine Zeitung, for Germany.

In contrast, selection of popular or tabloid format newspapers was more difficult. In countries, with mass circulation tabloids, such as Bild in Germany and The Sun in the UK, these were taken. In countries, without tabloids but with newspapers with a high circulation and a format that was more popular-oriented than the broadsheets, we took these, such as De Telegraaf in the Netherlands and El Mundo in Spain. Another selection problem with regard to tabloid/popular and regional newspapers came from France.

In France, Ouest-France, our chosen regional newspaper is actually the largest circulation newspaper nationally, overall, and could have been our popular newspaper, for which there is no clear candidate. In the end, we took L'Humanité as a fourth paper, which is distinct from broadsheet newspapers, but has a low circulation, and is politically close to the Communist Party. Due to this specificity L'Humanité was not included categorised as a tabloid/popular for the cross-newspaper analyses. A few country-specific problems remained.

For Italy, where regional North/South divisions are a key political cleavage, and where there were no clear candidates for mass circulation popular newspapers, we decided that it would be more representative of the newsprint landscape to select two regional papers (one northern La Nazione from Tuscany, and one southern Il Mattino). More problematic still was Switzerland, where politics is strongly regionalised at the cantonal level, and there is a languagebased cleavage.

To represent the Swiss newsprint landscape, we selected the two main official language communities, French-speaking and German-speaking, and took a broadsheet from each of centre-right affiliation Neue Zürcher Zeitung and Le Temps, and two popular newspapers, Blick and Le Matin. In addition to these national and sub-national newspapers, we added four transnationals, targeted largely at elite and business readerships.

Here we selected the Financial Times (Europe), the European versions of two American transnational newspapers, the International Herald Tribune, and the Wall Street Journal Europe. In addition, we took the weekly European Voice which has a limited circulation, but is directed specifically at a readership among the EU-level Brussels elite. All four transnationals are in English. Interviews were made with only the editors/leaderwriters and EU correspondents for the transnational papers, as the other categories of journalist were not relevant.

Plus the transnationals were included only at the interview stage. A further alteration was necessary from our original plan with respect to the UK. For Britain we originally selected and coded The Sun. However, The Sun took an editorial-level decision not to collaborate with our project, even refusing to allow its journalists to speak with us. It is, of course, a finding that the newspaper considers its own stance on Europe to be so politically sensitive, that it refuses to collaborate with academics, particularly when it has collaborated in previous projects on sensitive public issues such as immigration.

However, this was not helpful to the comparative aims of our study. We therefore replaced The Sun, with its mass circulation tabloid rival The Mirror, which is traditionally more left-leaning politically, and often takes the opposite stance. Such a decision allowed us to include a UK tabloid for the interviews.

Interviews of one hour duration were undertaken in 2003/4, initially face-to-face and where not feasible by telephone. All were recorded and stored. Each national team undertook their interviews and coding, meaning that interviewees were addressed in their own language and cultural context. Teams were very diligent in their recruitment attempts achieving 110 interviews out of a total possible of 120 (112 national and regional, 8 transnational).

Our interview schedule is systematically structured: it contains many questions with closed answers, but also spaces for the interviewee to expand more openly on the given answer. Due to time constraints not all interviewees answered all questions, plus not all questions were relevant for all types of journalist, which account for the varying 'n' in presented tables. Questionnaires for transnational actors were modified where necessary.

Responses to closed questions were coded numerically into a data-base for comparative analyses, in a way that is linked to relevant qualitative information from open ones. This strategy allows us to retrieve linked quantitative and qualitative information, selected by country, or newspaper or journalist type.

We acknowledge the limitations in selecting four newspapers to represent a national newsprint landscape, and-four journalists to represent political coverage by a newspaper, however, decisions were taken by experts within each country to provide a selection that best fitted our categories for functional equivalents, and allow comparative analysis across three dimensions. Overall, we consider the explanatory benefits of undertaking cross-national, cross-newspaper, cross-journalist analysis outweigh the limitations due to logistically necessary restrictions.

3

NEWSPAPERS AND CLAIMS-MAKING OVER EUROPE: AN OVERVIEW

Before examining factors which potentially drive coverage over Europe, it is necessary to build an empirical picture of the similarities and differences between newspapers, newspaper types, and countries. For this we use our contents analyses of journalists' claims-making acts in commentaries, and on claims-making acts in news reports.

First, for the media's representation of claims-making over political events, it is possible to calculate an overall position over Europe (ranging from -1 to 1) for 'all reported claims-makers', i.e. the claims and demands made by collective actors as 'third parties' reported in the news. Second, for the media's own claims-making, it is possible to calculate an overall 'position' score for each newspaper's own claimsmaking within commentaries with regard to Europe (ranging from -1 to 1).

By combining these dimensions we arrive at a political space with four possibilities for newspapers' positioning over Europe: pro-European representation and claimsmaking (top-right); Eurosceptic representation and claims-making (bottom-left); pro-European representation and Eurosceptic claims-making (top-left); and Eurosceptic representation and pro-European claims-making (bottom-right). This is shown for the newspapers aggregated by country and newspaper type.

We consider the perpendicular distance from this equilibrium to be an indicator for the extent of the media's autonomy, i.e., the extent to which a newspaper makes efforts to express a stance over Europe that is independent from the position which derives from its established organizational culture within the newsprint landscape.

In addition, the media's autonomous 'voice' pushes in a pro-European (below the line) or Eurosceptic (above the line) direction relative to its representation of political affairs.

The newspapers from all countries except Britain, and all types of newspapers except for L'Humanité (other), cluster in the top-right political space, which indicates pro-European representation and claims-making. Cross-nationally, we see that there is relatively little difference in the ways that claims-makers are represented (vertical distance) which is with an aggregate pro-European stance.

The main differences are in the stances taken by newspapers over Europe (horizontal distance). Here the German press comes across as the most pro-European, followed by the Netherlands, France, Switzerland and Spain which are pro-European but exhibit less autonomy than the Germans in advocating pro-European stances. At the other pole, the British press exhibits considerable autonomy to advocate Eurosceptic stances relative to other countries. The Italian press is intermediary in that it exhibits autonomy and advocates a stance that is more Eurosceptic than its representation of political affairs, but overall remains favourable to Europe.

In summary, for advocacy over Europe there seems to be a difference in national press culture between Britain at one pole, which exhibits more autonomy of expression and a Eurosceptic tendency, and Germany, at the other, followed by the rest, which have a clear pro-European stance but are relatively less assertive. Italy comes between.

Interestingly, leaving aside L'Humanité (below), we find few cross-newspaper-type variations in the way that newspapers make claims over Europe (horizontal distance), and they are all mildly pro-European. The limited differences we find are that broadsheets are more pro-European in their representation of claims-makers than popular and tabloid formats (vertical distance).

This is likely to be an outcome of the greater space their formats give to elite actors, and that advancing European integration is an elite-driven project. Regional newspapers which are more likely to give space to collective actors from two policy fields that are central to advancing Europe, agriculture and regionalism, are the most pro-European newspaper type in their representation of political discourse.

Finally, centre-left and centre-right broadsheets are virtually identical in their claims-making and representation of claims-making over Europe, which implies that a broadsheet's political affiliation on the left/right axis is not decisive in shaping its European coverage.

The only newspaper which represents the political discourse in a way that gives an overall Eurosceptic position is the British tabloid The Sun, whereas the only ones that take an aggregate claims-making stance which is at all Eurosceptic are, in order of their Euroscepticism: The Sun, L'Humanité, The Times, The Scotsman, and La Repubblica.

This underlines that in general newspapers tend to commentate over and report on political affairs in a way that is more likely to promote pro-European rather than Eurosceptic positions.

Overall, regarding newspapers' autonomy, we find relatively limited levels, with the newspapers' own claims-making in most cases remaining close to its representation of other actors' claims-making. We interpret this to mean that in most cases newspapers remain within their organisational culture and make only limited additional efforts to take a stance over European issues. There are notable exceptions. The Swiss tabloid Blick is an unequivocally strong pro-European advocate, followed to a lesser extent by the German broadsheet Süddeutsche and French Le Temps. Others which are pro-European but not in a way that is autonomous from their overall representation of reported political reality are, in order of their pro-Europeanism: Ouest France, De Volkskrant, Het Algemeen Dagblad, Le Figaro, Le Monde, FAZ, Bild, La Vanguardia, De Telegraaf, and Il Corriere della Sera.

At the other end of the scale, the Communist newspaper L'Humanité has a lot of autonomy and is a strong Eurosceptic advocate. L'Humanité represents the political discourse in a way that is no more Eurosceptic than other French newspapers, but its own claims-making advocates the Euroscepticism of the Communist party with which it is strongly affiliated. The Sun is also a strong Eurosceptic advocate. It is the strongest Eurosceptic claims-maker even going beyond its own strongly Eurosceptic organisational culture. Given that The Sun decided at the editorial level that none of its journalists could participate in our study because of the issue's sensitivity, we suggest that The Sun is exceptional in that it deliberately promotes Euroscepticism, both by political advocacy and in the way that it represents political discourse, which is considerably more Eurosceptic than the other British newspapers. Another newspaper from the Rupert Murdoch stable, The Times, is also strong Eurosceptic advocate, but as a newspaper of public record, it represents the political discourse in a similar way to The Guardian. Overall, The Sun and The Times and to a lesser extent The Scotsman make our British sample exceptional cross-nationally in that.

However, apart from The Sun, their representation of political reality with regard to European affairs does not greatly vary from other countries. Finally, perhaps surprisingly, the Italian La Repubblica and Il Mattino exhibit autonomy and advocate positions that are more Eurosceptic than their coverage of claims-makers.

In general, it is difficult from contents analysis to infer what may account for observed variations that are produced by actors, which is why we also undertook systematic interviews. An answer to this Italian puzzle came from our interviews (see below).

INTERVIEW FINDINGS: DRIVING EUROPEAN COVERAGE?

Readership's Demand

To address the impact of readership's demand for information on European coverage, we asked journalists from national and regional newspapers to assess their readerships' interest and understanding of European politics compared to politics in general. On a four point scale (not at all = 0, a little = 1, moderately = 2, greatly = 3), journalists consider their readerships to be less interested in European politics (1.5) than politics in general (2.2), and that readers have a low understanding of the workings of European politics (1.1). This perception holds cross-nationally, and across newspaper and journalist type.

The perceived reasons for low readership interest are the complex nature of European politics, that readers' interpretative frameworks for 'national' politics are strongly established, and due to deficits in the supply of political information over Europe. These are considered important barriers to readerships' comprehension. Typical responses are: 'They are still more interested in national politics: there the frontiers are stronger clear-cut, the conflicts more controversial, the actors better-known and the impact on their own life is bigger.' (Home Affairs Journalist, FAZ). '(Interested in European politics?) 'Not very much. Not as much as they should be, but that's cause they're not told much about it.'

(Martin Kettle, Chief Leader Writer, Guardian). 'They are too complex to become popular. It is a complex process of institutionalization that escapes most people's understanding.' (José Antonio Zarzalejos, Director, ABC). The journalists' comments demonstrate that they think readerships lag behind in their understanding of the importance of Europe in political affairs. On these findings, readership's demand for political information is likely to reduce rather than increase the extent to which newspapers cover Europe, and readership preferences for national politics and interpretative frameworks will restrict the potential for journalists to produce 'multi-leveled' or supranational accounts.

By comparison, the eight journalists from transnational newspapers felt their readerships had a greater interest in politics (2.8), and especially European politics (2.8), and a higher understanding of the workings of EU politics (1.9), compared to the national and regional press. This difference is attributed to the specialist nature of their readerships, which for the FT and European Voice are political and economic elites who have more international outlooks and need to keep informed about global affairs: 'The FT's big strength... is the emphasis we put on the relationship between business and politics. That is something that our readers (mainly business people) prize very highly.' (Brian Groom, Editor, FT Europe)

COLLECTIVE ACTORS' AGENDA-BUILDING

To address the supply-side influence of collective actors' agenda-building on European coverage, we asked journalists about the frequency with which they are confronted by the 'source strategies' by political actors. We aimed to establish the scope and type of collective actors targeting information at journalists.

Our key finding is that journalists face communication strategies from national actors, who, as we discussed earlier, have vested interests in advancing national interpretative frameworks. Four 'national' collective actors are ranked in the top five source strategists. 'National' governments are the only actor who 'regularly' (2.0) targets journalists whereas 'national' interest groups (1.8), political parties (1.7) and campaign and protest groups (1.3) come second, third and fifth, respectively. This underlines the importance of agenda-building attempts by national actors compared to regional, European and (non-European) supra-, transnational and international ones.

Overall we see a hierarchy by scope of national actors, followed by regional, and then European and international ones. Within the different levels of politics, our findings confirm expectations that institutionalised and powerful actors target journalists more than non-institutional, independent and less conventional types. However, from the perspective of national and regional newspapers, EU and international actors make feeble attempts to directly influence coverage. The European Union institutions (1.4) are the only actor above the nation-state who makes noteworthy communication efforts.

This makes the EU a source strategist only on a par with national campaign and protest groups (1.3), and regional and local governments (1.2) and interest groups (1.2). European interest groups (0.8) and protest groups

(0.6) make very few efforts to influence the national and regional domestic press by mobilising information at all. This means that even the limited information targeted at journalists from Europe will promote 'institutional' rather than wider 'public' or 'civil society' perspectives.

Looking at differences between journalist types, we see that European institutions target EU correspondents considerably more often (2.3) than they do 'normal' journalists (national 0.8; regional 1.1). This shows that the EU directs its communications at the topical specialists more than the mainstream. The low extent to which the EU addresses agriculture and immigration reporters is perhaps surprising, given that the EU is an influential actor in both policy fields, especially agriculture. By contrast, national governments target EU correspondents (1.9) and normal journalists (national 2.0; regional 2.1) at similar levels. Overall, it seems the EU makes little effort to compete with national actors to influence 'normal' beat journalists.

Generally, we find only a limited development of European 'source strategies' targeting the national and regional press, and these are from the EU institutions. Our enquiries with journalists from the transnational press reveal interesting variations. These journalists receive more information mobilised by European institutions and political parties, and international institutions, than from national and regional ones.

In addition, there is some limited evidence for source strategies by European interest groups and protest and campaign groups. Such findings support the idea of a 'restricted' Europeanisation of the public sphere, catering for specialised transnational political and economic elites (Schlesinger 1999), that is provided by transnational newspapers and to a limited extent within national and regional newspapers by specialist European correspondents.

ORGANISATIONAL CULTURE

To assess the influence of organisational culture, we offer some general findings from our interviews, and inquire specifically about journalists' self-perceptions about the media's role. On organisational culture, our interviewees emphasise the importance of 'editorial line' within newspaper organisations. This is not openly discussed, but 'internalised' as a set of implicit professional norms and organisational practices into which journalists are socialised. This editorial line defines the limits of political expression and influences the level and style of coverage over Europe. The Guardian's Chief leader-writer's comments are illustrative: 'I am the custodian of the Guardian's institutional position that has evolved over decades. The Guardian is historically an internationalist paper and pro-European. It is sympathetic to moves which involve Europe.

That's where we're coming from. If I believed, which I don't, that Britain should have nothing to do with Europe, then I couldn't write those leaders.' To examine journalists' general view of what the media's role on Europe should be, we asked them about the EU's perceived 'democratic deficit' and whether the media should aim to reduce this by informing and educating the public. On a four point scale (from 'no role at all' 0 to 'an important role' 3), our 94 respondents considered the press have a 'moderate role' (2.0) to play in reducing the 'democratic deficit'.

Some are critical of the media's performance: '(The) Media can do it a lot but the problem is how they do it. They are a little behind, they don't give much importance to the EU and they are not clear about EU.' (Paolo Garimberti, Co-Director, Repubblica). However, comments indicate that journalists perceive the 'democratic deficit' to be a problem within institutional politics, i.e., the political system and not the media system.

They think the media should expose such perceived 'deficits', but are clear that this is an informative not a political role. Journalists tend not to see the 'democratic deficit' as their responsibility, nor do they adopt 'pioneering' normative stances over it: 'The media are no substitute for Parliamentary control' (EU Political Journalist, FAZ), 'To discuss, explain, verify (journalists) can help people to understand the importance of the EU. Nevertheless, EU decision-making lacks transparency. EU Commissioners are perceived as not politically responsible because they are not elected.' (Paolo Garimberti, Co-Director, Repubblica). '(On perceived role re: democratic deficit) We're a commercial organisation so it's not our job. I do believe there is a democratic deficit, and it's an interesting topic and we try and cover it.' (George Kerevan, Associate Editor, Scotsman). 'There's generally a low understanding of the functioning of EU institutions, only the newspapers can fill this gap.' (Sgnr. Yarnuz, Correspondent, El Pais). Overall, the 'democratic deficit' is seen as an important topic but not as a justification for transforming existing journalistic practices and norms, nor as an opportunity for an enhanced political role. The transnational papers share this stance with the exception of the European Voice, which acting as the paper for the transnational Brussels elite is more proactive on the transparency of the EU, but this is within its editorial line. '(W)e to try and make up for the fact that EU institutions, generally speaking, aren't exactly models of transparency, by trying to put as much information that the people in important positions want to keep secret, in the public domain.' (David Cronin, EV, Political Correspondent).

INFRASTRUCTURE, INFORMATION GATHERING AND SELECTION

First, with regard to infrastructure we find very little evidence for organizational efforts to transform news production processes and journalist practices specifically to enhance European coverage. Newspapers have responded to the challenge of reporting European affairs in an 'ad hoc' way. They try to incorporate Europe as a 'topic' into pre-existing news gathering and reporting practices. New posts for European correspondents tend to occur as a branch of foreign affairs. Changes within the organisation to cover Europe are usually at the initiative of a few key individuals and not a response to an institutional concern. Overall the limited innovations by national and regional dailies have been responsive and evolutionary rather than proactive and transformative. Even the transnational press are less pro-active in generating European transnational perspectives than one might expect, as Brandon Mitchener WSJE outlines: 'With the notable exception of the Wall Street Journal and the European Voice, all other major media tend to treat Europe as a collection of nation-states, and EU affairs do not get as high a profile as national news... most journalists ... they'll only write about it if it's important to their country."

Journalists' information gathering and selection practices are also likely to be influential factors for European coverage. First, there may be special considerations in gathering information for European affairs, such as the availability of organizational resources for research and investigation, or a journalist's own knowledge, or alternatively, access to official documents, experts' knowledge, or citable public figures. Second, Europe may be difficult to fit within existing 'news values' and formats, because of its 'difference' as a complex, technical issue, or as an emergent type of event with a multi-levelled scope, or because of its perceived incommunicability, due to lacking charismatic spokespersons, or clear cues from politicians. Thirdly, there may be special 'news desk' concerns over Europe, such as competition for news space or the pressure of deadlines, or Europe could be an issue over which journalists face pressures from editors, or the news organisation's management to advance a specific position. To construct a general picture of the relative importance of these factors facing journalists.

Generally, we see strong cross-national similarities showing that journalists from different countries see themselves as facing similar problems. Journalists are especially concerned about the availability of news space (2.5) and the necessity to capture audience attention (2.0). This holds across newspaper and journalist type. Journalists' comments assist interpretation. Overall, they emphasise difficulties fitting 'European' stories within existing 'news values', formats and space requirements. Such news selection problems arise from the type of political events, their complexity, and from the flow and type of information 'sources' from Brussels, which are obscure, remote from domestic politics, and lacking in the qualities -e.g., few 'conflicts between personalities'- that would increase 'news values' and enhance their perceived relevance and communicability to readerships. Problems of limited space also result from the nature of the issue, as one interviewee explains, 'The main problem regarding stories of the EU is the complexity of the EU issues.

A journalist has to explain much more. This results in problems of space.' (Agricultural Correspondent (Brussels), FAZ). Most journalists share such views: 'When writing stories about Europe it is even more difficult and complicated to break down the issue into an understandable form' (Chief Editor, Blick); 'It's difficult to get anything in about the Common Agricultural Policy. CAP is mainly figures, if you could make it into personalities or have an element of conflict then that would help. All the newsdesk are interested in is 'are they having a fight or not'?' (Fordyce Maxwell, Rural Affairs Editor, Scotsman); 'In general it is difficult to get an item on Europe in the paper, as it is regarded as boring, and there is too little debate about it.' (Hetty Van Rooij, European Correspondent, Leeuwarder Courant); 'The space is not sufficient for EU issues. Because of that we don't deal on a daily basis with EU issues. It is necessary to be able to explain things well to the reader. Extreme synthesis cannot be made on very technical and complex things' (Roberto Giardina, EU Correspondent, Nazione).

Within this common viewpoint, we find some cross-newspaper variation. Journalists from popular (3.0), tabloid (2.7), and regional (3.0) newspapers find the news space factor especially problematic compared to the broadsheets (centre-left 2.4; centreright 2.0). In addition, tabloid journalists (2.4 compared to 2.0 for all) find it harder than other types to capture the audience's attention for Europe. On this Bild's political editor elaborates: 'It is difficult to access the relevant actors and it is difficult to convert European issues into the language of BILD. There are no photos of Europe because the actors are unknown.' Even journalists from transnational newspapers concur: 'I think it's the language and understanding issue. Europe is constructed in such a way that ... is too complex for the average European. It doesn't resemble anything on the national level, and the decision-making is opaque.' (Thomas Fuller, IHT.)

At the other end of the scale, institutional pressures from within the news organisations are clearly not especially problematic. Pressure from the management and the organisation (0.4), and pressure from senior editors and journalists (0.7), rank lowest.

Between these poles, some but not all journalists mention information gathering issues, such as, access to 'sources' of expert knowledge, and official documents and public figures, and to resources for investigative research. For example, 'we cannot do investigations, we do not have not enough resources to have someone working for a week on an issue' (Socio-Economic News Editor, L'Humanité). 'Access: I can't cover the Justice and Home Affairs council of the EU because it is closed to the media. I can't even get hold of the papers until several months after they've been discussed.'

(Alan Travis, Home Affairs Editor, Guardian), 'EU institutions based in the UK don't go out of their way to make themselves known and amenable to journalists. The Commission office in London was "exceptionally unhelpful" in a query about the possible change to the EU flag.' (Alison Hardie, Political Correspondent, Scotsman).

One important aspect of information gathering is journalists' relationships with EU institutions as a 'source'. Here we examined the perceived quality of the EU's communication strategies compared to national political actors, with whom they compete to attribute meaning to events.

Specifically, we asked about the EU's information supply with regard to: its information-provision performance, its 'objective' or neutral qualities of suitability for news, such as providing usable material for news copy, accurate information, or specialist knowledge expertise; and its political-communicative performance, its 'political' qualities of suitability for news, such as providing a clear political line, political transparency, and opportunities for discussion.

Generally, journalists consider the EU s overall professional standards (-0.2) to be slightly worse than national actors. Also the EU's information-provision performance is clearly better than its political-communicative one. The EU's specialist knowledge/expertise provision (0.1) is rated 'better' than national actors, compared with openness to discussion (-0.2), transparency (-0.3), and having a clear political line (-0.4) that are 'worse'.

Journalists' comments clarify that the EU's communication is substantially different from national actors. On information-provision performance, many journalists mention the EU's technocratic style, its complexity due to the number of countries and issues involved, and the remoteness of EU actors and their press office. A typical remark is: '(It is) Worse because there is a huddle of competences in Brussels, where different nations follow their different interests. Additionally the way of life in Brussels is not very conducive: It seems many have lunch between 11 a.m. and 4 p.m. and then go home.' (Bonn Correspondent, Bild). Some criticise the suitability of information received, 'The most stupid are the service of spokesmen and Eurostat that fax 30 pages of numbers as if we have time to figure it out' (EU Correspondent, Ouest France). 'They (European institutions) say 'take the whole thing and look for the focus', the national ones say 'take 2 sheets, it's our focus, and if you like I'll then give you the whole thing'.' (Pedro Simón, Editor, El Mundo). Others appreciate the expertise of the information, especially on agriculture, and that it is less likely to be delivered with 'political spin': 'They try to give a lot of info and they try less than national governments to dodge issues by using "stiff talk" (langue de bois).' (Socio-Economic News Editor, L'Humanité). 'Less spinning here.' (Rory Watson, Brussels Correspondent, Times).

Apart from this, most aspects of the EU's political-communicative performance compared to national politicians are seen as problematic, especially transparency and the absence of a clear political line. Typically, one journalist remarks: '(T)here is less openness, less transparency and I cannot see a clear political line.' (Editor, Leipziger Volkszeitung). This general negative view holds more for the Commission than the European Parliament, where the existence of political cleavages and party politicians, helps journalists to report political messages: 'The people (means MEPs) who are motivated and understand how to sell politics, who are operating through the Parliament are very good. The (EU) institutions are bad.' (Lorraine Davidson, Brussels Correspondent, Mirror).

Transnational journalists share the views of their colleagues from national and regional newspapers over the EU's communicative performance. For example, Brandon Mitchener (WSJE) criticised the Commission but respected the press officers representing political parties and lobby groups in the European Parliament: 'The main thing is that the Commission tends to ... hire experts, who are very good at their subjects, but have zero idea how the press works, and which strings to pull to get a good quote or a good spin on a story in a newspaper or a radio interview.'

MEDIA AGENDA-SETTING AND ADVOCACY

Another important factor potentially influencing European coverage is journalists' own agenda-setting efforts. Here we sought to underpin the findings from our contents analysis. Specifically, we focussed on commentating as the journalistic practice which allows most scope for directly advancing opinions and evaluations in the attempt to exert political influence (Eilders and Voltmer 2003). First, we aimed to determine the extent to which journalists attempt to influence actors external to news production processes, when commentating on politics, and second, the type and scope of these actors. We take this as a general indicator for advocacy.

Generally, journalists seem to have only limited advocacy ambitions, and target their public audience more than political institutions and collective actors. Their own readerships (2.3) are the only constant target, followed by national public opinion (1.7), and informed public opinion, 'the chattering classes' (1.7). After this, national political actors are the next most significant: national government (1.6), national-political parties (1.3), and national interest-groups (1.3). The findings show clear hierarchies for the addressees of journalists' advocacy, by actor type and scope. First, overall they are more likely to try to influence institutional actors (1.1), than interest (0.8) and campaign and protest groups (0.6). Second, within this, journalists target national, then regional, followed by European and international actors.

Again, this underlines our previous findings, that journalists see national institutionalised politics as the most important. It is striking that journalists attempt to influence the European Union institutions only 'from time to time' (0.9), to the same extent as regional and local interest groups, and even less than regional governments (1.2). Even the newspapers' specialists on European affairs, EU correspondents, attempt to address national governments (1.3) and political parties (1.3) more than EU institutions (1.1), which have the same score as regional governments (1.1). In sum, we find limited political advocacy efforts by national and regional newspapers toward political actors and these attempts prioritise national over supranational European politics. Transnational newspapers are similar in the limited extent to which their advocacy addresses the political system, and deviate slightly from national and regional papers in that European institutions are targeted to the same extent as leading national governments. The only exception is the European Voice which makes concerted advocacy efforts with regard to European supranational actors.

A second thrust of our inquiry was to gauge whether and how journalists' political commentating differed when covering European affairs in comparison the national affairs. Here we examine the nature of the media's own advocacy, specifically, whether it has informative-educative or partisan qualities, and whether it has the potential to shape European affairs.

To address this, we constructed a set of possible differences that could vary when journalists commentate over European rather than national affairs. Some differences were 'internal' to journalists' writing, such as whether 'national interest' becomes more prominent as an issue, whether the educative role relative to the readership is enhanced due to limited public knowledge over the topic, whether independence to express a political stance increases, and whether more effort is made to influence political elites. Others were 'external', such as, whether newspapers are more likely to follow an established party political line, or that of the proprietor, or that of national public opinion. After establishing an overall aggregate picture of differences, we drew from journalists' open comments on the most important difference to add qualitative contextual detail.

Table 5 shows the rankings and overall aggregated scores for journalists' perceived differences when commentating on European compared to national affairs, on a scale from 0 for the lowest, to 3 for the highest difference. Differences by subcategories of journalist type are also given, as these are more striking than cross-national or crossnewspaper differences.

In general, journalists do not see considerable differences in commentating on Europe, with the highest perceived difference being 1.7 on a scale from 0 (no) to 3 (yes). In addition, we have a clear negative finding with regard to differences that are 'external' to journalists' writing practices. The political stances of proprietors (0.5), political parties associated with the newspaper (0.4), and general public opinion (0.3), are not more of a consideration when commentating on Europe. From this we deduce that the way that journalists comment over European affairs is not an outcome of extra pressures placed on them to follow their proprietors', political allies', or general public's position over Europe perceived flow of opinion-leading is from journalists to external political actors, i.e. from the media system to the political system.

It is also worth noting that this holds especially for journalists writing for popular (express own position 2.1, mean 1.4; influence political elites 2.1, mean 1.3) and tabloid newspapers (express own position 2.3, mean 1.3; influence political elites 1.7, mean 1.3) than for broadsheets and regionals. However, this is more likely to be an outcome of the generally more assertive commentating style of popular and tabloid newspapers, than a factor specific to commentating on Europe. One cross-national variation concerns Britain, however, where journalists are more inclined to follow the proprietor's position over Europe than elsewhere (1.0 compared to 0.5 mean). This 'exception' comes from the Times' journalists, which as a member of the Murdoch group appears to have a clear editorial line over Europe that is enforced within the organisation, to a greater extent than other newspapers.15 Overall though, journalists seem to be as free to write in their political commentaries over Europe as they are over national affairs.

Turning to the limited differences between commentating on European and national affairs, these are 'internal' to writing practices for political commentary. These give us an indication of the type of advocacy by journalists over Europe. First, journalists mention their likelihood for promoting opinions that defend 'national interest' (1.7), which is again evidence for journalists' national interpretative frameworks over Europe. Second, they emphasise that they have an informative and educational role and duty to improve public knowledge (1.6), which is stressed more than attempting to influence political elites (1.3). Overall this points in the direction of informative-educative advocacy and raising awareness over Europe, more than partisan advocacy and ideologically-based activism.

This interpretation is strongly supported by journalists' comments on the greatest difference when commentating over Europe. As they did for reporting, journalists emphasise difficulties that are specific to communicating about Europe as topic, much more than any perceived difficulties in attributing it a specific ideological bias. By far the overwhelming difference that journalists mention is the need to explain and express more clearly, and in more detail, because of the lack of public and readership knowledge about European compared to national affairs: 'There's an attempt to explain things better when the EU level is spoken of, it's a task of giving more clarity, knowing that the reader isn't as familiarised with the EU's functioning compared to national politics.' (Andrés Ortega, Editor, El Pais).

'On European issues (we) have to be a lot more informative since more explanations are needed for the reader to understand the opinion piece.' (Pedro Cuartango, El Mundo) 'The public does not know much about the subject so the paper has the duty to inform.' (Rimmer Mulder, Editor, Leeuwarder Courant). 'The newspaper sees itself as pro-European, internationalist, it feels it has duty to inform and explain because of levels of ignorance of the subject and the failings of government over the EU.' (Ian Black, European Editor, Guardian). These examples, selected from many, underline that journalists see the key difference when commentating on European affairs to be the need to inform and educate the public and their readerships. It emphasises the informative-educative much more than the partisan dimension of journalists' advocacy over Europe.

However, an important difference is that journalists consider they have a greater scope to comment more openly over European politics, because political cleavages are not as clearly established in the political system and public imagination as they are for national politics: '(There is) bigger freedom to express opinion because there is less conditioning from national political actors or political groups.' (Alessandro Farruggia, Agriculture Correspondent, Nazione). 'At the national level, there is more interest in the standpoints of the political parties, which can be overcome at the European level, (thus we are) less partisan concerning Europe.' (Sgnr. Gonyáley, El Mundo). 'European affairs are commented on with more freedom as party politics is not important. On a national level, trenches of party politics dominate. There are a lot of prejudices.' (EU Correspondent, FAZ). For the most part, this greater independence for political expression over Europe is an outcome of the lack of established cues and clear positions from the political system, and is not perceived as an opportunity by journalists to give ideological leadership in political debates over European affairs. In the large majority of cases, they see themselves as responding to a political void by raising awareness.

One exception to this overall trend is the Swiss tabloid Blick which takes up an educative-informative and partisan stance to the extent that it even goes against its understanding of its own readership's position over Europe: 'The most important thing is that the Blick writes against its public when it comes to European politics; it does it consciously, rather than writing as its public thinks' (Chief Editor). This underpins our contents analysis' findings with regard to Blick's exceptional pro-European advocacy. Apart from this, however, the greater assertiveness of popular and tabloid journalists remains within the same norms and parameters as it does for commentaries on national affairs. As a Mirror journalist states: 'I don't think there is much of a difference (between Europe and national), (we are) fairly strident on both UK and European issues. We would rant and rave about foundation hospitals as well as rant and rave about why we need to get into Europe.' Thus even tabloids and popular newspapers are mostly informative-educative about Europe, raising awareness for understandings within their own established organisational culture, rather than being partisan ideologues over Europe.

On the Italian press, our contents analysis showed a surprisingly high level of autonomy for advocacy that overall is favourable to Europe, but more Eurosceptic than newspapers' representations of political affairs. From our interviews it seems that this apparent ambivalence toward Europe derives from the Italian press advocating pro-Italian interests within European affairs -which may be either for or against European integration- rather than simply advocating pro-European positions. As one journalist states: 'In commentating on national politics, we take positions without prejudices. On EU politics there is the tendency to bring to the European level Italian reasons for wishing that a common Italian position is brought in,' (Mario Orfeo, Director, Il Mattino). Thus the Italian press consciously push for an Italian version of Europe, but this may go either for or against different aspects of European integration.

Turning to cross-journalist variations in Table 5, we see that all four highest perceived differences are more distinctly expressed by EU correspondents than either editors/leader-writers or national and regional journalists (defend national interest 2.0, mean 1.7; improve public knowledge 2.1, mean 1.6; express own position 1.7, mean 1.4; influence political elites 1.6, mean 1.3). Again, the duty for improving public knowledge is especially strongly emphasised. This indicates that European correspondents appear to be a distinct group among journalists with a specific set of norms. They take on a specialist role as pioneers commentating on Europe but once more this advocacy role is perceived as informative-educative and raising public awareness for European issues. Findings on the transnational newspapers go in a similar direction. In general,-journalists feel they have fewer constraints than their national and regional colleagues for commentating due to being located transnationally, rather than being tied to national politics, and by virtue of having a diverse readership: "We don't have an owner who has an agenda, we don't have an editor who has an agenda, we have a peculiar purpose which is to be the forum for all sorts of different views, which a national newspaper sometimes can't afford because their role is to address a certain constituency within a national system, and we don't have, our constituency is so broad that we'll give them all the views." (Thomas Fuller, Brussels Correspondent, IHT).

For the FTE, WSJE and IHT, this perceived independence for expression does not lead to partisan advocacy, but remains informative-educative. Editorials on Europe are often written at the domestic newsdesk, even in the US or Britain.

By contrast, the weekly European Voice operates more like a national newspaper for the supranational EU politics and serves Brussels. This organisational culture promotes an editorial line for independent and critical views directly addressing European Union affairs: '(E)ditorial policy has definitely changed... the paper was a little bit too cosy with the European Commission... I think people now know what we are about.

So, for instance, whistleblowers come to EV now, which they might not have in the past, but then so do prime ministers and presidents, when they want to write an op-ed, which they didn't in the past. If you come across as a serious independent-minded newspaper, more people are likely to take it seriously.' (Dennis Abbott, Editor, EV). Again, although the European Voice promotes Europe, it acts as a forum for opinions from a range of views, and is directed more at informing than contesting.

In summary, we find little evidence for journalists using commentaries for partisan purposes over Europe. This is underlined by the overwhelmingly negative responses to our questions about whether the newspapers ran political campaigns over Europe. In the few cases of media campaigns, these tended to be one-off issue-specific attempts and not the adoption of a consistent ideological position over Europe, such as the Bild's and Il Mattino's attempts to raise awareness about price rises resulting from adopting the Euro currency. Generally, commentating on Europe and the scope for journalists to express overt political positions seems to operate within the limits set by the perceived editorial line and the newspaper's organisational culture.

It is mainly knowledge deficits and the emergent and relatively undefined nature of European politics which allows journalists the freedom to express opinions, not that they see themselves as advocates with a political axe to grind.

CONCLUSION

To our knowledge this chapter presents one of the first attempts to study the contribution of journalism to 'Europeanization' by recourse to systematic empirical evidence on factors external and internal to the news production process, ranging across seven countries from the European region. Much remains to be done, but we hope that these findings present a general base-line from which others can undertake more detailed studies on specific countries, or types of journalism, or aspects of the news process. Thus we highlight some main findings. Our contents analysis shows that most newspapers produce pro-European positions, both in the way they represent the political discourse and contribute to it through commentary.

On this aggregated evidence, it is hard to see the press as a source of Euroscepticism, as it is often accused of being by politicians. On the contrary, to the extent that opinions are shaped by mediated discourse, the press can be considered to be generally supportive of European integration. The Sun, of course, is an exception, but was the only newspaper to be an outright advocate of Euroscepticism to the extent that this also shaped its representation of politics. Also, the British press' commentating at one pole, is to a limited extent more Eurosceptic than the German press', at the other, though there are overall few differences in the way that countries represent political reality, which is perhaps surprising given that Euroscepticism is more salient in British politics.

Also we generally find relatively low levels of media 'autonomy', where a newspaper's own position varies from its representation of politics, the exceptions are the Eurosceptic Sun, Pro-European Swiss tabloid Blick, and the French Communist Party's Eurosceptic L'Humanité. Overall, newspapers seem not to wander from their established organisational culture over Europe. The cumulative evidence from our interviews adds detail and gives explanatory support to this perspective. Outside the news production process, readership's preferences for national politics and low understandings of Europe act as a restricting condition for journalists' efforts to present 'multi-leveled' or supranational interpretative frameworks. Also the feeble efforts of EU-level collective actors to target information at the press, compared to their strong national competitors' agenda building activities, again limits the possibilities for 'Europeanised' coverage.

Factors within news production processes tell us about the media's response to the political changes brought by advancing Europeanisation, and journalists' selfperceptions of their practices, and the media's obligations and role.

Regarding organisational responses, overall the limited innovations by national and regional dailies are 'ad hoc' and evolutionary rather than pro-active and transformative. Even the transnational press are less pro-active in generating European transnational perspectives than one might expect. 'Europe' is basically incorporated as a topic into pre-existing news gathering and reporting practices. Thus the 'democratic deficit' is important as a topic to journalists, but not as a motivation for transforming the media's role.

Responsibility for remedying any such shortfalls in political communications is left squarely on the shoulders of elected politicians. Journalists quite consciously distinguish between the media and political systems and do not see Europe as opportunity for extending their own political role. Nonetheless, clear differences and challenges exist in covering European affairs from the perspective of the journalist as a practitioner. These mostly arise from the nature of the subject matter which does not fit easily into established news values and reporting practices. Journalists have problems with the political-communicative qualities of the EU's information rather than its supply. EU politics is hard to fit into the immediate, visible, personalised, conflict-based narratives that cover national politics, and so finds space harder to come by. Thus EU actors suffer relative to their national counterparts within European coverage and nationalised viewpoints tend to predominate.

Interestingly, these same particularities of European politics, give journalists more individual freedom to express opinions when writing commentaries, compared to national affairs. However, this is an outcome of a lack of established cues and positions from the political system, and not perceived as an opportunity for giving ideological opinion-leading. Journalists mostly see themselves as responding to a political void by raising awareness. We find their own agenda-setting efforts targeting their own readers, and to a lesser national governments, with the EU hardly registering. Overall, journalists see their advocacy over Europe as a way of informing and educating the public by raising awareness. There is very little evidence for ideologically motivated advocacy, or the media seeing itself as a political actor. For the most part, advocacy remains within the limits of a newspaper's established editorial line in the media landscape. This means that newspapers' positions tend to reflect similar levels of uncertainties and inconsistencies to those built around the cleavage structure over Europe in national political systems. Stated simply, the media system tends to follow the political system over Europe, it 'represents' much more than it 'leads' political debate.

In general, we find strong cross-national similarities in journalists' perceptions. This indicates that Europeanisation is experienced as impacting on different national press cultures in similar ways. There appears to be a 'universal' experience of Europeanisation within journalism. Among journalists, EU correspondents are pioneers, who create a possible forum for more Europeanised viewpoints within the limits set by their restricted structural location in the newspaper. Among newspapers, the transnationals have a similar limited emergent role within structural restrictions. Such findings support the idea of a 'restricted' Europeanisation of the public sphere (Schlesinger 1999), catering for small transnational political and economic elites, mediated by transnational newspapers, and to a limited extent within national and regional newspapers by European correspondents. Any further future Europeanisations of political journalism are likely to start from there.

4

POLITICAL JOURNALISM IN AMERICA

INTRODUCTION

These pages tell the story of an experiment. It began early on 1995, when Ed Fouhy and Jan Schaffer of the Pew Center for Civic Journalism encouraged the formation of media partnerships in various locations around the country in hopes of discovering better ways to cover election campaigns. The main focus was to be on the 1996 presidential primaries and caucuses. By late spring five partnerships had been formed in four states - New Hampshire, Iowa, Florida and California - and Fouhy had recruited me to be executive director of what we soon decided to call the Citizens Election Project.

In time, the project grew to include two additional partnerships (in Iowa and North Carolina), plus the California Voter Foundation's online election guide. The CEP sponsored major undertakings by two Washington, D.C.-based opinion-analysis companies, The Harwood Group and the Pew Research Center for the People and the Press, and contracted with Washington public relations firm of Neuman & Co. to handle outreach and press relations. We also arranged with the Nieman Foundation at Harvard to conduct weekend seminars on how the principles of civic journalism might improve campaign coverage. Much as these various elements of the CEP differed from one another, they shared a common assumption: That something was radically wrong with political journalism in America, and that if journalists themselves didn't do something to correct the problem, they might awake one morning to discover that their fellow citizens were no longer paying any attention to them at all.

The point cannot be overemphasized. Although civic journalism has been dismissed by some misinformed critics as "boosterism" or "political activism," it is, as this report makes clear, nothing of the kind. Civic Journalism simply seeks to reconnect journalists to the people they have always claimed to serve - readers, listeners and viewers who want to be informed about the world they live in. That the connection over the past several years has been damaged, if not utterly destroyed, is a fact that many journalists have come belatedly to accept. The CEP experiment was an attempt to demonstrate, in the context of political reporting, ways in which the connection might be rebuilt.

The Washington Post's wise and trenchant media columnist Richard Harwood (no relation to the president of the Harwood Group) has written:"Some of the critics of 'civic journalism' - inadvertently, perhaps - suggest that the only true and legitimate journalist is a strange species of citizen who betrays himself and his 'calling' if he harbors notions of civic responsibility or cares about the purpose and impact of his work. It is a species, fortunately for democracy, that exists in very small numbers if at all."

The best journalists, Harwood suggests, have never been uninterested in the moral and political implications of their work, and to the extent that they are uninterested today, they place their craft - perhaps even the political system- at grave risk.

In addition to the work done by The Harwood Group, the Pew Research Center for the People and the Press and the California Voter Foundation, the Citizens Election Project consisted of the following media partnerships, all of which were mostly self-sustaining but which received funding from the CEP for specific purposes that fell outside normal editorial budgets:

IOWA

Two CEP partnerships used distinctly different approaches to the Iowa caucuses. The first involved the Iowa-based Lee Newspaper chain, Iowa Associated Press, plus radio and television outlets. They sponsored a series of six town meetings and a debate by GOP presidential candidates. The other gave Iowa high school students an opportunity to question candidates on statewide closed-circuit television.

NEW HAMPSHIRE

There were two CEP partnerships in the Granite State as well. One was based in Boston and followed the town of Derry, N.H. (pop., 30,000) and its citizens through the entire New Hampshire primary season. Among other things, this partnership conducted extensive polling and focus groups in Derry and sponsored local forums. The second New Hampshire partnership was statewide and was notable for a series of question-and-answer meetings it arranged and covered between small groups of citizens and the GOP presidential candidates.

FLORIDA

The largest of the CEP's partnerships, this one included most of the major newspaper and television outlets in the state, plus radio station WUSF-FM and WSFP-FM. The group conducted two important statewide polls and sponsored a town-hall meeting prior to the Florida straw poll in November.

CALIFORNIA

A San Francisco-based partnership produced a series of articles about nine Bay Area neighborhoods, reporting the problems those neighborhoods, reporting the problems those neighborhoods faced and the attitudes of the residents on the eve of the San Francisco mayoral election in the fall of 1995. In addition, the partnership co-sponsored two highly successful candidate debates during the mayoral campaign. The debates featured questions from citizens and from a panel of political reporters.

In this report on the CEP's activities, you will read articles by key people involved in each of the partnerships and by Andrew Kohut of the Pew Research Center for the People and the Press and Kim Alexander of the California Voter Foundation in Sacramento. You will not, I think, find any boosterism or political activism. Rather, you will encounter the reflections of serious people who, recognizing that their projects were experiments, have frankly assessed what they did right and what they - we - did wrong. You will also discover a pride in having taken part in something that gave many of the participants a substantial edge over journalists elsewhere when it came to assessing which issues were of most importance to voters in the four key states where CEP projects existed.

Last March, after the race for the Republican presidential nomination had seemingly been decided in favor of Sen. Robert Dole, the New York Times published a major series of articles on the issue of "job security." It was almost as if the Times, like Dole, had discovered that the issue was important only after seeing another GOP contender, Pat Buchanan, use it successfully in Louisiana, Iowa and New

Hampshire. But, as several of the reports in this publication make clear, if other journalists had taken the trouble - as the CEP partners did - to listen carefully to what people were saying before the campaign reached its superheated stage, they would have known months earlier that job security was an issue, perhaps the issue. Indeed, the 15 focus groups that The Harwood Group conducted for the CEP in Iowa, New Hampshire, Florida and California had revealed the same trend as early as September, 1995. (See America's Struggle Within, a Harwood Group report issued by the CEP in January 1996, specifically, Chapter II, "A Nation off Course.")

In general, then, the Citizens Election Project was a major success when it came to gauging the views of the voters and helping them (as opposed to the politicians and the media) set the agenda for the campaign. Failure occurred in some areas when the partnerships were forced to rely on the candidates' cooperation. As you will read here, a few town meetings either had to be cancelled or scaled back when the front-running candidates decided, for reasons best known to themselves, to boycott them. The events were citizen-driven, completely nonpartisan and unscripted - and it appears to have been precisely those elements that scared away the front-runners. In this era, when candidates believe that the ticket to victory is to do say as little as possible, it may be naïve to assume that they will cooperate simply to help raise the level of political discourse.

In any case, there is some feeling among the CEP partners that the time has probably arrived when civic journalism projects in the political arena ought to move beyond candidate forums and develop new ways of achieving the same ends. Over the long term, reform of political journalism will not rely so much on special projects or special events as on the development of new attitudes and frames of reference by political reporters and their editors all over America. What is needed, above all, is a realization that treating voters as if the only time they really matter is when they actually cast their ballots or reply to some pollster's questions is to miss the whole point of the electoral process and to play directly into the hands of the media manipulators who today have so much control over the process.

That is another way of saying that civic journalism will have come of age when it is no longer compartmentalized and no longer experimental but is part of the warp and woof of every journalist's experience. On that day, the "civic" may be dropped altogether, and we will be back to plain old good journalism again.

5

ADVERTISING AND PROMOTION IN POLITICAL JOURNALISM

You may have the finest product and the most attractive prices, but if potential customers don't know about your business, your chances of success are limited. Advertising and promotion refer to activities undertaken to increase sales or enhance the image of a product or business. Advertising is used primarily to inform the potential customer of (1) the availability of products or services, (2) when they are in season, (3) where you are located and (4) anything special about your product.

Promotional activities are important for maintaining customer traffic throughout the market season-used early in the season to draw customers to your business and during the season to maintain customer traffic levels during slow periods.

Unfortunately, the benefits of advertising and promotion for direct farm marketers have yet to be consistently demonstrated. Promotion of farm products appears to be effective in some cases, but not in others. The potential for successful advertising and promotion is increased when products are clearly differentiated, are of exceptionally high quality, are very seasonal in nature or are new offerings.

Research conducted on direct farm marketing indicates that advertising, with emphasis on product freshness and quality, is more likely to move produce than price eutting.

How much should you spend? It is considered good business in retail marketing to spend 2 to 3 percent of gross sales for advertising. A 1985 survey of direct farm marketers in the mid-Atlantic states showed that producers spent an average of 3 percent of sales on advertising. You may find you cannot afford to do as much advertising as you would like. Therefore, it is important to set priorities. A scattered shotgun approach with limited funds usually ends up with poor results. It is important to plan your advertising program, otherwise you may fritter away your hard earned dollars. Know your targeted customers and direct your appeals to them.

BE HONEST AND FACTUAL

On-farm and roadside markets with that "something special" usually build their merchandising program around a distinguishing trademark-a unique sign, display, atmosphere or building design. Advertising is easier to remember and more appealing when backed up by a unique, easily illustratable business name or slogan that clearly and concisely states the nature of the business and/or the principle products sold, e.g., WILBER'S WATERMELONS, APPLE ANNE'S-Fruit, Cider, Bakery Goods, RATZLAFF'S CHEMICAL FREE PRODUCE. Avoid creative names that may serve to confuse your potential customer. Many successful on-farm businesses carry the owner's name, creating a more intimate and sincere relationship with the consumer.

In the summer of 1993, a survey was undertaken of the fresh farm produce outlets in Cochise County, Arizona. Visitors were asked how they learned about the direct farm market they were patronizing. A similar survey was completed in Michigan. The results, summarized as follows, give some indication of the effectiveness of different-promotional activities. Let's now look at each of these promotional activities and how they might be used in your enterprise. To help you evaluate these advertising options, first ask yourself: Why am I considering doing this? What is it suppose to do? What are my goals? Then seek feedback from your customers, particularly new customers, as to how they heard about you, to determine which advertising media was most effective.

Word-of-mouth

What can you do to help your present customers spread the word? Provide visitors with your business card. Include fliers or coupons with each purchase and ask your customers to pass them on to family and friends. Develop and distribute "point of purchase" marketing materials and displays:

A "Fresh Farm Produce" buyers' guide and map (discussed later). Information on "how to" pick, reduce spoilage, can, freeze, dry produce, etc.

Recipes and Cooking Ideas

How to get to other farm outlets and community points of interest. Build repeat customers through customer satisfaction. Inquire into the customer's needs. Seek suggestions for improvement. If visitors have a bad experience or don't find what they were looking for, they not only don't return, but will also tell others where not to stop.

Maintain a guest register or ask customers to fill out a pre-printed card. Then mail them a postcard or flier at the start of next year's season thanking them for their business, indicating when different produce will be available and inviting them back. Hopefully they will also bring others. Consider having customers register directly on to a postcard. Later, print your message on the reverse side. This can save you a lot of time.

Media Coverage

The fresh farm produce outlets in the Willcox, Arizona area have been particularly successful in generating and receiving news coverage in local and regional newspapers and television. Not only has this media coverage been very effective in promoting the outlets, it is free. The direct farm marketers in an area should consider banding together to generate media publicity. Name (contract with) a publicist to develop media opportunities and systematically generate positive publicity for the area's direct farm marketing outlets. This might be done through the local Chamber of Commerce. Organize a media tour of area outlets. Invite the media to special events.

(a) Classified ads in the food or for sale sections of the Want Ads of local and regional newspapers: The ad should indicate what is for sale, when and where. Most direct farm marketers do not advertise price.

(b) Display ads in the entertainment or food section or in special supplements of regional newspapers: Such ads should be attractively designed and easy to read, with a limited number of words and a good use of white space. Incorporate a trademark or symbol in every ad so that it is quickly recognized by your regular customers. The advertising department of the newspaper can help you plan a layout. Since such ads are more expensive, cooperative funding should be explored with other area direct farm marketers. A group ad will convey to potential customers the wide variety of outlets, produce and experiences available, and assure visitors that they are likely to get what they want if they make the trip.

(c) Radio ads: Due to their higher cost, spot announcements on the radio must be short and to the point, 15 to 30 seconds. More frequent short announcements are believed to reach more people than less frequent longer ones. Frequent spot announcements can help create name recognition.

(d) Place information articles and/or advertising in area shopping guides, tourist publications, company and special interest news-letters targeted to specific audiences, e.g., Garden Clubs, health food, retirement communities, ethnic food.

(e) Yellow pages listing.

Roadside Signs

Road side signs are a particularly important information source once travelers are near your business or event. Road side signs can be hindrances if they are not done professionally and kept well maintained. If signs are unattractive, hard to read, home painted and unkept, your operation is likely to start with a bad impression.

The entrance to you business should be clearly marked with a pull-off area on each side of the road. Your initial road sign should, as a rule, be placed

at least 2,500 feet from the entrance to your business to allow travelers a safe stopping distance. Then place several advance road signs out from your initial sign that state the distance to your business, e.g., JONES' PRODUCE, 2 MILES. Signage should start from the nearest Inter-state or major highway and clearly direct visitors to your business location. Roadside signs should contain six words or less, with a 1 or 2 word focal point to catch the traveler's interest.

Use 7" to 12" letters and a good contrast of colors. The most easily read color combinations are black, dark blue, bottle green or scarlet red on white, yellow, orange or green. It is not always the size of the letters that make them readable, but the space or margins around them. Create a simple logo, such as the example provided, that provides easy recognition.

Media Advertising

There are a number of options for media advertising. Interviews with direct farm marketers indicate that the most commonly used mediums are:

Community Brochure/buyers' Guide

Many rural communities have developed an informational brochure or directory that lists all direct farm marketers in the area with a description of the products they offer. Also included is a map of the area with directions to each outlet and a harvest calendar indicating when different fruits and vegetables will be available. Such brochures are often developed with the aid of the county Cooperative Extension office and are funded through a subscription of those businesses listed.

Printing and financial aid may also be available through a local utility or the state Department of Agriculture. Such directories will be effective, however, only if they are properly promoted and distributed to prospective customers. The printing cost of the brochure is small compared to the cost of promoting the directory, postage for mailing them and travel costs in placing the directory at travel information centers and brochure racks at strategic locations. This directory should also be distributed at the direct farm market outlets to assist with referrals and encourage return visitors and word-of-mouth promotion. This project might be coordinated by the local Chamber of Commerce.

The Willcox community has implemented a telephone service which out-of-town customers can call for a regularly updated recording indicating produce availability. The service is sponsored through subscriptions from the advertised businesses.

Referrals

Make sure that the employees of recreation and tourist facilities, motels, gasoline stations, restaurants, campgrounds, the Chamber of Commerce and other visitor oriented businesses are aware of your business. These people can help channel more customers to you. Make referrals.

Exchange customers. Help visitors find the products they are looking for. The Cochise County survey found that many visitors were not aware of the wide diversity of products available at other locations. Some returned home without purchasing sought-after items. When asked what other products or activities they would like to see offered, a significant number of visitors indicated a park/picnic area, swimming, horseback riding, a good place to eat-not knowing that those facilities were available in the Willcox community. A community brochure and map to local restaurants, museums, motels, retail shops, swimming and other recreational facilities should be available at the farm outlets.

Special Festivals

Agricultural festivals can be effective in attracting visitors to your community. They can generate additional sales if on-site activities are provided which bring potential customers in contact with your products. Such on-site activities might include things like hay rides, pick your own pumpkin (or watermelon), menudo cook-off, celebrity tomato pitch, watermelon seed spitting contest and farm tours. Unfortunately, the research indicates that limited spending on fresh farm products occurred at agricultural festivals mainly because such products (even those that the festival was named after) were not widely available. The festival activities- often interfered with visitors getting to-local businesses and on-farm outlets.

Special Tours

Field trips and special tours have proven effective in bringing people to the area and your business that might not have made it on their own.

Such groups include garden clubs, residents of retirement communities, ethnic clubs, foreign visitors and company picnics. School tours have been effective in stimulating return visits by the children with their parents in tow.

Coupons, Special Discounts, Drawings

Experience indicates that general discounting can be counter productive in the direct marketing of farm produce. A discounted price suggests lower quality. The use of coupons can, however, help you track the effectiveness of different advertising media.

In general it is recommended that discounts be expressed in whole dollars and cents rather than as a percent, and focus on increasing business during the slow seasons of the years. Giving your valued customers on unexpected benefit, e.g., free samples of new or slow moving produce may have a more positive impact than a discount.

Labels

Labels on bags, boxes, jars and containers reinforce your name to the consumer. Labels provide an opportunity for word-of-mouth advertising as guests to your customers' home observe your products. Generally, people will buy food items as gifts only when there is an attractive label indicating its origin and special qualities. Also labels can be effective in promoting the quality of your product, e.g., vine ripened, pesticide free, organic, high fiber, farm fresh, vitamin rich. Your name, logo and/or- slogan can also be printed on T-shirts, aprons, hats and bags, for sale, to help your customers promote your business.

ADVERTISING AND PROMOTIONS MANAGER

- Prepare budgets and submit estimates for program costs as part of campaign plan development.
- Plan and prepare advertising and promotional material to increase sales of products or services, working with customers, company officials, sales departments and advertising agencies.
- Assist with annual budget development.
- Inspect layouts and advertising copy and edit scripts, audio and video tapes, and other promotional material for adherence to specifications.
- Coordinate activities of departments, such as sales, graphic arts,. media, finance, and research.
- Prepare and negotiate advertising and sales contracts.
- Identify and develop contacts for promotional campaigns and industry programs that meet identified buyer targets such as dealers, distributors, or consumers.
- Gather and organize information to plan advertising campaigns.
- Confer with department heads and/or staff to discuss topics such as contracts, selection of advertising media, or product to be advertised.
- Confer with clients to provide marketing or technical advice.

- Monitor and analyze sales promotion results to determine cost effectiveness of promotion campaigns.
- Read trade journals and professional literature to stay informed on trends, innovations, and changes that affect media planning.
- Formulate plans to extend business with established accounts and to transact business as agent for advertising accounts.
- Provide presentation and product demonstration support during the introduction of new products and services to field staff and customers.
- Direct, motivate, and monitor the mobilization of a campaign team to advance campaign goals.
- Plan and execute advertising policies and strategies for organizations.
- Track program budgets and expenses and campaign response rates to evaluate each campaign based on program objectives and industry norms.
- Assemble and communicate with a strong, diverse coalition of organizations and/or public figures, securing their cooperation, support and action, to further campaign goals.
- Train and direct workers engaged in developing and producing advertisements.
- Coordinate with the media to disseminate advertising.
- Contact organizations to explain services and facilities offered.
- Direct and coordinate product research and development.
- Represent company at trade association meetings to promote products.

- Consult publications to learn about conventions and social functions and to organize prospect files for promotional purposes.

Requirements:

- Bachelor Degree in Commerce, Marketing or Administration.
- Minimum of 7 years experience.
- Strong English language skills. Including the meaning and spelling of words,
- Knowledge of principles and methods for showing, promoting, and selling products or services. This includes marketing strategy and tactics, product demonstration, sales techniques, and sales control systems.
- Knowledge of media production, communication, and dissemination techniques and methods. This includes alternative ways to inform and entertain via written, oral, and visual media.
- Knowledge of principles and processes for providing customer and personal services. This includes customer needs assessment, meeting quality standards for services, and evaluation of customer satisfaction.
- Knowledge of business and management principles involved in strategic planning, resource allocation, human resources modeling, leadership technique, production methods, and coordination of people and resources.
- Knowledge of design techniques, tools, and principles involved in production of precision technical plans, blueprints, drawings, and models.
- Knowledge of raw materials, production processes, quality control, costs, and other techniques for

maximizing the effective manufacture and distribution of goods.

- Knowledge of administrative and clerical procedures and systems such as word processing, managing files and records, stenography and transcription, designing forms, and other office procedures and terminology.

PRINCIPLES OF MARKETING

Advertising

In the next five sections of the Principles of Marketing Tutorials we begin an in-depth look at each promotional mix item. In this tutorial we present the first of a two-part examination of advertising with a discussion of basic concepts and trends. Our coverage of advertising continues in our next tutorial, Managing the Advertising Campaign, where we look at what decisions are needed to carryout a successful advertising campaign.

In this tutorial we cover several fundamental issues in advertising including examining what advertising is and why it is important to the marketing organization. We also look at managing the advertising effort by comparing in-house management to that offered by advertising professionals, such as advertising agencies. Finally, the tutorial identifies different types of advertising and addresses trends facing the advertising industry.

What is Advertising?

Advertising is a non-personal form of promotion that is delivered through selected media outlets that, under most circumstances, require the marketer to pay for message placement. Advertising has long been viewed as a method of mass promotion in that a single message can reach a large number of people. But, this mass promotion approach presents problems since many exposed to an advertising message may not be within the marketer's target market, and thus, may be an inefficient use of promotional funds. However, this is changing as new advertising technologies and the emergence of new media outlets offer more options for targeted advertising.

Advertising also has a history of being considered a one-way form of marketing communication where the message receiver (i.e., target market) is not in position to immediately respond to the message (e.g., seek more information). This too is changing.

For example, in the next few years technologies will be readily available to enable a television viewer to click a button to request more details on a product seen on their favorite TV program. In fact, it is expected that over the next 10-20 years advertising will move away from a one-way communication model and become one that is highly interactive.

Another characteristic that may change as advertising evolves is the view that advertising does not stimulate immediate demand for the product advertised. That is, customers cannot quickly purchase a product they see advertised. But as more media outlets allow customers to interact with the messages being delivered the ability of advertising to quickly stimulate demand will improve.

Importance of Advertising

Spending on advertising is huge. One often quoted statistic by market research firm ZenithOptimedia estimates that worldwide spending on advertising exceeds (US) $400 billion. This level of spending supports thousands of companies and millions of jobs. In fact, in many countries most media outlets, such as television, radio and newspapers, would not be in business without revenue generated through the sale of advertising.

While worldwide advertising is an important contributor to economic growth, individual marketing organizations differ on the role advertising plays. For some organizations little advertising may be done, instead promotional money is spent on other promotion options such a personal selling through a sales team. For some smaller companies advertising may consist of occasional advertisement and on a very small scale, such as placing small ads in the classified section of a local newspaper.

But most organizations, large and small, that rely on marketing to create customer interest are engaged in consistent use of advertising to help meet marketing objectives. This includes regularly developing advertising campaigns, which involve a series of decisions for planning, creating, delivering and evaluating an advertising effort. We will cover advertising campaigns in greater detail in our next tutorial.

Managing Advertising Decisions

Delivering an effective marketing message through advertising requires many different decisions as the marketer develops their advertising campaign. For small campaigns, that involve little creative effort, one or a few people may handle the bulk of the work. In fact, the Internet has made do-it-yourself advertising an easy to manage process and has especially empowered small businesses to manage their advertising decisions.

As we will see, not only can small firms handle the creation and placement of advertisements that appear on the Internet, new services have even made it possible for a single person to create advertisements that run on local television. For instance, a company called SpotRunner allows users to select from a list of high-quality television ads that can be customized and then placed within local cable television programming.

For larger campaigns the skills needed to make sound advertising decisions can be quite varied and may not be easily handled by a single person. While larger companies manage some advertising activities within the company, they are more likely to rely on the assistance of advertising professionals, such as those found at advertising agencies, to help bring their advertising campaign to market.

Advertising Agency Functions

Professionals at advertising agencies and other advertising organizations offer a number of functions including:

- Account Management - Within an advertising agency the account manager or account executive is tasked with handling all major decisions related to a specific client. These responsibilities include locating and negotiating to acquire clients. Once the client has agreed to work with the agency, the account manager works closely with the client to develop an advertising strategy. For very large clients, such as large consumer products companies, an advertising agency may assign an account manager to work full-time with only one client and, possibly, with only one of the client's product lines. For smaller accounts an account manager may simultaneously manage several different, though non-competing, accounts.
- Creative Team -The principle role of account managers is to manage the overall advertising campaign for a client, which often includes delegating selective tasks to specialists. For large accounts one task account managers routinely delegate involves generating ideas, designing concepts and creating the final advertisement, which generally becomes the responsibility of the agency's creative team. An agency's creative team consists of specialists in

graphic design, film and audio production, copywriting, computer programming, and much more.

- Researchers - Full-service advertising agencies employ market researchers who assess a client's market situation, including understanding customers and competitors, and also are used to test creative ideas. For instance, in the early stages of an advertising campaign researchers may run focus group sessions with selected members of the client's target market in order to get their reaction to several advertising concepts. Researchers are also used following the completion of an advertising campaign to measure whether the campaign reached its objectives.
- Media Planners - Once an advertisement is created, it must be placed through an appropriate advertising media. Each advertising media, of which there are thousands, has its own unique methods for accepting advertisements, such as different advertising cost structures (i.e., what it costs marketers to place an ad), different requirements for accepting ad designs (e.g., size of ad), different ways placements can be purchased (e.g., direct contact with media or through third-party seller), and different time schedules (i.e., when ad will be run). Understanding the nuances of different media is the role of a media planner, who looks for the best media match for a client and also negotiates the best deals.

Types of Advertising

If you ask most people what is meant by "type" of advertising, invariably they will respond by defining it in terms of how it is delivered (e.g., television ad, radio ad, etc.). But in marketing, type of advertising refers to the primary "focus" of the message being sent and falls into one of the following four categories:

Product-Oriented Advertising

Most advertising spending is directed toward the promotion of a specific good, service or idea, what we have collectively labeled as an organization's product. In most cases the goal of product advertising is to clearly promote a specific product to a targeted audience. Marketers can accomplish this in several ways from a low-key approach that simply provides basic information about a product (informative advertising) to blatant appeals that try to convince customers to purchase a product (persuasive advertising) that may include direct comparisons between the marketer's product and its competitor's offerings (comparative advertising).

However, sometimes marketers intentionally produce product advertising where the target audience cannot readily see a connection to a specific product. Marketers of new products may follow this "teaser" approach in advance of a new product introduction to prepare the market for the product. For instance, one week before the launch of a new product a marketer may air a television advertisement proclaiming "After next week the world will never be the same" but do so without any mention of a product or even the company behind the ad. The goal is to create curiosity in the market and interest when the product is launched.

Image Advertising

Image advertising is undertaken primarily to enhance an organization's perceived importance to a target market. Image advertising does not focus on specific products as much as it presents what an organization has to offer. In these types of ads, if products are mentioned it is within the context of "what we do" rather than a message touting the benefits of a specific product. Image advertising is often used in situations where an organization needs to educate the targeted audience on some issue. For instance, image advertising may be used in situations where a merger has occurred between two companies and the newly formed company has taken on a new name, or if a company has received recent negative publicity and the company wants to let the market know that they are about much more than this one issue.

Advocacy Advertising

Organizations also use advertising to send a message intended to influence a targeted audience. In most cases there is an underlying benefit sought by an organization when they engage in advocacy advertising. For instance, an organization may take a stand on a political issue which they feel could negatively impact the organization and will target advertisements to voice their position on the issue.

Public Service Advertising

In some countries, not-for-profit organizations are permitted to run advertisements through certain media outlets free-of-charge if the message contained in the ad concerns an issue viewed as for the "greater good" of society. For instance, ads directed at social causes, such as teen-age smoking, illegal drug use and mental illness, may run on television, radio and other media without cost to organizations sponsoring the advertisement.

Advertising Trends

Like most areas of marketing, advertising is changing rapidly. Some argue that change has affected advertising more than any other marketing function. The more important trends in advertising include:

Digital Convergence

While many different media outlets are available for communicating with customers, the ability to distinguish between outlets is becoming more difficult due to the convergence of different media types. In advertising convergence, and more appropriately digital convergence, refers to a growing trend for using computer technology to deliver media programming and information. Convergence allows one media outlet to take advantage of features and benefits offered through other media outlets. For instance, in many areas around the world television programming is now delivered digitally via cable, telephone or satellite hookup. This delivery method uses the same principles of information delivery that is used to allow someone to connect the Internet.

The convergence of television and Internet opens many potential opportunities for marketers to target customers in ways not available with traditional television advertising. For example, technology may allow ads delivered to one household to be different than ads delivered to a neighbor's television even though both households are watching the same program. But convergence is not limited to just television. Many media outlets are experiencing convergence as can be seen with print publications that now have a strong web presence. The future holds even more convergence opportunities. These include outdoor billboards that alter displays as cars containing geographic positioning systems (GPS) and other recognizable factors (e.g., GPS tied to satellite radio) pass by or direct mail postcards that carry a different message based on data that matches a household's address with television viewing habits.

Focus on Audience Tracking

The movement to digital convergence provides marketers with the basic resources needed to monitor user's activity, namely, digital data. Any media outlet that relies on computer technology to manage the flow of information does so using electronic signals that eventually form computer data. In simple form, electronic data is represented by either an "on" or "off" electronic signal.

In computer language this is further represented by two numbers "0" and "1" and, consequently, is known as digital information. All digital information can be stored and later evaluated. For media outlets delivering information in digital form, the potential exists for greater tracking and matching this with information about the person receiving the digital data. And tracking does not stop with what is delivered; it also works with information being sent from the customer.

For instance, as we noted earlier, by clicking on their television screen viewers will soon be able to instantly receive information about products they saw while watching a television show. This activity can be tracked then used in future marketing efforts.

Audience Concern with Tracking

While media convergence offers marketers more options for tracking response to advertisements, such activity also raises ethical and legal concerns. Many consumers are not pleased to learn their activities are being monitored when they engage a media outlet. Yet consider the following examples of how marketers are tracking users:

- *Television Viewing* - As we noted, the advent of digitally delivered television allows cable, telephone and satellite providers to track user activity through the set-top boxes connected to a subscriber's television. Future innovation will make the user television experience even more interactive and, consequently, open to even more tracking.

- *Television recording* - The days of television videotape recording are quickly coming to an end, replaced by recording using computer technology. A digitial video recorder (DVR), such as TiVo, can track users recording habits and, based on a viewer's past activity, make suggestions for programs they may want to record. Additionally, advertising services can program the DVR to insert special advertisements within a program targeted to a particular viewer.
- *Internet Spyware* - Downloading entertainment from the Internet, such as games, video and software, may contain a hidden surprise - spyware. Spyware is a special program that runs in the background of a user's computer and regularly forwards information over the Internet to the spyware's company. In some cases spyware keeps track of websites the user has visited. The information is then used to gain an understanding of the user's interests, which then results in delivery of special ads when a user visits a certain site.

Ad Skipping and Blocking

As noted above, television recording devices offer marketers tremendous insight into viewers' habits and behavior. Yet from the consumer side, the DVR is changing how people view television programs by allowing them to watch programming at a time that is most convenient for them.

Viewer convenience is not the only advantage of the DVR. The other main reason consumers are attracted to the DVR is their ability to quickly skip over commercials. Of course this presents major issues for advertisers who are paying for advertisements. As more DVR devices with ad skipping or even ad blocking features are adopted by mainstream consumers the advertiser's concern with whether they are getting the best value for the advertising money becomes a bigger issue. Advertisers who feel frustrated with television ad-skipping may opt to invest their promotional funds in other media outlets where consumers are more likely to be exposed to an advertisement.

Changing Media Choices

There is a major cultural shift occurring in how people use media for entertainment, news and information. Many traditional media outlets, such as newspapers and major commercial television networks, are seeing their customer base eroded by the emergence of new media outlets.

The Internet has become the major driver of this change. In particular, a number of important applications tied to the Internet are creating new media outlets and drawing the attention of many, mostly younger, consumers. Examples include:

- *Podcasting Audio* - This involves delivering programming via downloadable online audio that can be listened to on music players, such as Apple's iPod. Many news websites and even other information site, such as blogs, offer free downloadable audio programming.
- *Podcasting Video* - While audio downloading has been available for some time, the downloading of video to small, handheld devices, including cellphones, is in its infancy. Many television networks are now experimenting with making their programming available for download, albeit, for a fee.
- *RSS Feeds* - This is an Internet information distribution technology that allows for news and content to be delivered instantly to anyone who has signed up for delivery. Clearly those registering for

RSS feeds represent a highly targeted market since they requested the content.

- *Networked Gaming* - While gaming systems have been around for some time, gaming systems attached to the Internet for group play is relatively new and becoming more practical as more people move to faster Internet connections. This type of setup will soon allow marketers to insert special content, such as advertising, within game play.

For marketers these new technologies should be monitored closely as they become accepted alternatives to traditional media outlets. While these technologies are currently not major outlets for advertising, they may soon offer such opportunity. As these technologies gain momentum and move into mainstream acceptance marketers may need to consider shifting advertising spending.

Marketers should also be aware that new media outlets will continue to emerge as new applications are developed. The bottom line for marketers is they must stay informed of new developments and understand how their customers are using these in ways that may offer advertising opportunities.

Press Ownership

In 1923, there were 26 metropolitan daily newspapers in Australia owned by 21 proprietors. By 1950, the number had fallen to 15 metropolitan dailies having 10 owners.

By 1987, there were three major proprietors of the metropolitan dailies-the Herald and Weekly Times Limited (HWT), News Limited (News), and John Fairfax Holdings Limited (Fairfax)-as well as a small number of independent publishers with newspapers in one city, which shrank to two when News Limited took over HWT that year.

Metropolitan Press

Five companies own most of the newspapers of Australia. By far the biggest is News Limited which controls 68 per cent of the market (70 per cent of metropolitan newspapers and 30-35 per cent of all Australian newspapers measured by circulation). The next biggest, Fairfax, owns 21 per cent. They control all of the metropolitan press except for West Australian Newspapers (The West Australian, eight per cent) and Rural Press (Canberra Times, three per cent).

Regional Dailies

As with the metropolitan newspapers the majority of regional dailies are owned by the five biggest companies. Only four are owned by independent family-owned companies.

Table. Ownership and circulation of regional dailies 2004

Company	Titles	Circulation	% of total
APN	13	162,496	27.2
Fairfax	3	95,030	15.9
News Limited	4	137,028	23.0
Rural Press	9	127,292	21.3
WA Newspapers	1	5,746	0.9
Independent	616		
68,382	11.5		
Total	36	595,974	99.8

Source: Communication Update: Communications Law Centre June 2005

Suburban, Rural and Community Newspapers

Newspapers in these categories are also predominantly owned by 'the main companies, News Limited, APN and

Rural Press. Details of the circulation and ownership of each paper are listed in Communication Update a publication of the Communications Law Centre and in the appendix of the Australian Press Council Annual Reports.

Ownership Restrictions

The existing laws, restricting cross-media ownership between television and newspapers, have been in force since 1992. They were introduced with the intention of maintaining diversity in all forms of media and enhancing public access to a variety of viewpoints. Several failed attempts to reform these laws have been made since.

The controls are embodied chiefly through the Broadcasting Services Act. Where it impacts on the print media, that legislation restricts the holder of a commercial television licence or a commercial radio broadcasting licence from owning a newspaper in the same licence area. In essence, that means a television or radio station owner in a city such as Sydney or Melbourne cannot own a newspaper that also services that same area.

There are additional laws that restrict foreign ownership. They restrict aggregate foreign ownership of national and metropolitan newspapers to 30 per cent. Ownership by foreign individuals is capped at 25 per cent.

Shareholdings of portfolio investors are restricted to 5 per cent, but there is provision for applications to be made to allow higher levels. Aggregate foreign shareholding of provincial and suburban newspapers is held to 50 per cent. There are no cross-media or foreign shareholding restrictions placed on magazines, the ethnic community press or online information sites.

Because of the cross media rules, the owners of the major broadcast networks are separate from the metropolitan newspaper owners. The three major network owners are

PBL (Nine Network, except Perth & Adelaide); Kerry Stokes's group (Seven); and Canwest (Ten). APN as well as owning newspapers is a major owner of radio stations. Some other radio network owners (such as Southern Cross) also have small television interests.

The only restrictions on concentration of press ownership are contained in the Trade Practices Act, which sets out Australian anti-trust law and applies to all industries. Section 46 proscribes the abuse of monopoly power through predatory practices. Section 50 proscribes the attainment or increase of a dominant position in a market. However, these may be authorised if there is a public benefit in the take-over.

The Australian Competition and Consumer Commissioner's view is that the product market for the press is the newspaper industry, not all media, and that for most metropolitan newspapers the market is limited to the state concerned.

A report of a parliamentary committee in 1992 found no abuses of concentration and made no recommendations concerning initiatives to create new newspapers. However, all members of the committee agreed that "...concentration of ownership is potentially harmful to plurality of opinion and increases the potential risk that news may be distorted" and accordingly urged that the risk of further concentration "...should be minimised'.

The report seemed to accept that, if new newspapers were created, there would be a market battle that would result in only one newspaper emerging.

It recommended that the test in Section 50 of the Trade Practices Act be amended to return to the pre-1977 proscription of takeovers that would result, or be likely to result, in a substantial lessening of competition.

Proposed Changes to Ownership Restrictions

In 2006, the Federal Government released proposals that would result in substantial changes in laws that govern control and ownership of print media companies and assets. At the time of writing, the new rules have yet to be framed and placed before the Parliament.

Pressure to amend the laws has mounted because of the emergence of new forms of media - especially digital media that can be made available online or in mobile form - from convergence of different mediums and from increased diversity in some areas.

The centrepiece of the proposed new laws for print media is the removal of cross-media restrictions and the imposition of new rules that set minimum limits to the number of independent voices in any given market. The limit would be five independent newspaper, television and radio operators in metropolitan markets and four in regional markets. The proposal allows considerable room for consolidation, and could result in significant media industry takeovers.

Any such actions would be regulated by the Australian Competition and Consumer Commissioner under the general merger provisions of the Trade Practices Act. The Australian Communications and Media Authority would be charged with ensuring that transactions comply with diversity requirements and the minimum limits.

The plan would result in foreign ownership limits being scrapped, but the media industry would still be subject to the "sensitive sector" provisions of the government's foreign investment policy. Sensitive sectors have tighter restrictions for requiring permission from the Federal Treasurer to exceed a 15 per cent shareholding and also involve more rigorous examination processes for approval.

Economic Health

Print media companies have enjoyed five years of growing revenues. The largest impact has come from a marked increase in advertising sales.

Published financial accounts show that metropolitan newspaper publishers had, by 2005, fully recovered from less favourable conditions in the wake of the introduction of the Goods and Services Tax in July 2000 to reach a level where their operating margins generally were running near the peak levels of previous economic cycles. Gross profits typically were in the range 25 per cent to 30 per cent of revenues, up from low levels of under 20 per cent.

Regional newspaper groups have returned a steadier pattern of growth and margin maintenance during that period, not having suffered to the same degree in 2001 and 2002 after the introduction of the GST. Margins are in a 30 per cent to 40 per cent range.

A study by PricewaterhouseCoopers (Australian Entertainment and Media Outlook 2006-2010, August 2006), shows that total newspaper industry revenues were $5.1bn in 2005, 14 per cent higher than the level of 2001. They had slumped to $4.35bn in 2002. The survey predicts an annual rise of three per cent to $5.84bn in 2010. About three-quarters of revenues come from advertising, which is predicted to increase at an average annual rate of four per cent-amounting to between $150m per annum.

Desirable but missing data for future editions would be trends in the employment of journalists, both for the print and internet activities of the paper, and trends annually in pagination, that is, the average size of newspapers in terms of number of pages for particular days of the week.

Circulation revenues on an industry basis now amount to $1.3bn. They have experienced considerable fluctuation as the sales of newspapers decline and aggressive promotional subscription offers are made. After a drop of 9.9 per cent in 2001, circulation revenues have slowly turned around to be running about one per cent annual growth, a trend predicted to continue through 2010. There is considerable variance between metropolitan and regional newspapers, brought about by migration of people to Queensland and to coastal towns on the east coast. This spurs greater growth in many regional areas. The other main reason for the current circulation revenue rise is increase in cover price.

Magazines

Magazine publishers have also been recovering from a downturn that started five years ago, but they have rebounded faster than newspaper companies. Price water house Coopers reports that this segment grew by 6.1 per cent in 2005, when revenues exceeded $2bn for the first time.

It expects future revenue growth until 2010 to run at an average annual rate over four per cent. Revenues streams are evenly divided between advertising and circulation, although advertising is expanding slightly more rapidly. The main causes of circulation revenue growth are increased unit sales, revitalised categories, new titles and cover price rises.

The magazine industry covers a broad range of interests, from fashion to celebrity, special interest to news. The performance of any given category can vary significantly from year to year, with celebrity and fashion being two of the recent high growth areas. There has also been sizeable expansion in magazines that are inserted in newspapers. They enjoy wide distribution and have quickly attracted advertising support. It is a trend that is likely to continue.

The Industry

The improvement in the industry's financial health has resulted in an increased investment in news rooms, but the extent to which this occurring is difficult to quantify. Funds are being spent on newspaper and magazine websites in an attempt to capitalise on the rapid expansion in advertising through this medium.

Newspapers now frequently update their websites, with news stories written by members of staff through the day rather than running articles supplied by wire services. A considerable number of staff are devoted to the production of inserted magazines and lifestyle sections, some of which add to staff levels. Available total headcounts often show strong rises, but these are misleading because most major publishers in recent years have expanded by making acquisitions within Australia and overseas.

Advertising Revenue Trends

Advertising revenue has rebounded strongly in recent years, but its continued strength depends directly on domestic economic conditions. Some print media companies have recently cautioned that the outlook is weakening because of factors such as increased fuel costs. Consumer sentiment and retail spending are both displaying weakening trends, and they have a considerable impact on both advertising and circulation.

Newspapers

Total advertising expenditure in newspapers has been growing since 2002 at an annual amount reaching $300m. That reflects high single digit growth. Price wate rhouse Coopers predicts that this will moderate, but still continue at an annual rate around 3.5 per cent until 2010. About two-thirds of the growth comes from display advertising.

Display advertising makes up 57.6 per cent of the advertising stream, up from 52.3 per cent in 2002. To be most effective, display advertising requires full colour printing. That has become more widely available in recent years, allowing colour advertisements to run on many pages of a newspaper. Publishers are also focusing on inserts and the development of lifestyle sections and premium magazines, which open doors to new display advertisers. This trend should continue as newspaper companies sell more, higher margin colour display advertising. To this end, the major publishers have recently formed a new industry body to promote their colour printing capacities to advertisers.

Classified advertising, long known as "the rivers of gold" for newspapers such as The Age and The Sydney Morning Herald, is diminishing in importance as advertisers are attracted to online sites and specialist publications. According to the 2006 survey, Classified revenue grew by 1.4 per cent to $1.6bn (compared with the 2.2 per cent overall growth in newspaper advertising). In 2002 classifieds accounted for 47.7 per cent of advertising in newspapers; this share is now down to 42.4 per cent.

Magazines

Magazine advertising grew by 9.3 per cent in 2005. One reason for this was the strong increase in circulation, enhancing magazines' attractiveness as an advertising medium. The 2006 survey predicts growth at about five per cent for the rest of the decade, outpacing the predicted growth in newspaper advertising revenue.

The Industry

The largest threat for advertising comes in the form of competing online sites. Consumers are spending more time using the internet and advertisers are finding new ways to reach them, either by placing advertisements on those sites or by supporting search engines. A global report by Boston Consulting Group (Finding the Sweet Spot in Online Search, July 2006) says that the time consumers spent between 1999 and 2004 on newspapers, magazines, radio and television rose or fell by just a couple of percentage points. But time spent on the Internet escalated by 24 per cent. Online advertising expenditure rose by 22 per cent, whereas traditional media spending declined.

A similar trend is evident in Australia. Price water house Coopers says that Internet advertising in 2005 topped $500m for the first time, reaching $620m, compared with $160m in 2001. It expects annual growth exceeding 20 per cent for the rest of the decade, with revenues reaching $1.78bn by 2010. The annual dollar expansion in the near term is predicted to be around $200m. That is about the same dollar growth expected for newspapers. On the other hand, UK media buyer Group M has recently estimated that Internet advertising this year will beat for the first time advertising in national newspapers in that country. The online trend is particularly impacting print media's grip on classified advertising. The three core categories of internet advertising, general, classifieds and search & directories, each experienced strong growth in 2005 and now have a relatively even share of revenue. Search & directories had the greatest growth and now surpass classifieds as the main category.

With the widespread adoption of broadband, the Internet could also have a negative effect on display revenues. Estimates provided by stockbroking company ABN Amro suggest that employment advertisements online currently account for an estimated 20 per cent of the market, and it is the largest single classified advertising sector. Real estate comes next, with online accounting for about 10 per cent, and cars come third at around eight per cent.

6

MEDIA PLURALISM AND POLITICS IN DEMOCRATIZING SOCIETIES

For the past quarter-century, many countries around the globe have been transitioning from governments with centralized control of authority to some form of democracy. There are several types of democracy, of course, and these transitioning countries have engaged various strains, stages, and ideals along the way. Nevertheless, many countries in Latin America, Eastern Europe, Africa, and Asia can be described as somewhere along the continuum from "transitioning" to "post-transition democratizing" societies.

One building block of democracy that has assumed heightened attention in recent years is the role of civil society. Civil society is the nongovernmental, non-business element of the public sphere, often informal, that many people believe is essential to a healthy democratic society. One amino acid of a strong civil society, at least in industrialized countries, is a pluralistic press.

That diversity of views, sources, and ownership, the theory goes, enables a marketplace of ideas to emerge and democracy to flourish. But is media pluralism an essential element to create a civil society in a transitioning state in which tradition, culture, governmental attitudes, and economic conditions are so different? If so, in what ways? And how does one sustain such pluralism in the face of many obstacles along the path to a free, democratic society? Variously, governments are new, jealous, or fragile. Markets are tenuous, fractious, and often weak or, conversely, virulent and inclusive of semi-governmental competitors or illegitimate players. Non-profit organizations are nascent, foundations non-existent, and a tradition of civil society absent. Furthermore, the general public often is unaccustomed to critical analysis of the varied content coming from a variety of news sources.

INTRODUCTION

In 1974 a global "third wave" of democratization began when a military coup in Portugal ended the dictatorship of Antonio Salazar, who himself had come to power in a military coup in 1926. Over the course of the succeeding 15 years, about 30 countries changed from various forms of nondemocratic regimes to nominally democratic ones, most dramatically in South America and Central and Eastern Europe.

During this period, notable transitions from nondemocratic rule also occurred in Africa and Asia. The questions still confronting many of these nations are whether their transitions are permanent or passing and, if the former, what obstacles lie in the way of democratic consolidation.

Perhaps the largest obstacle, asserts political scientist Samuel Huntington, is the recognition that "democracy is a solution to the problem of tyranny, but not necessarily to anything else." Poverty, ethnic and racial conflict, inadequate economic development, chronic inflation with substantial external debt, and political leaders—many of them former dissidents—who are not fully committed to the democratic ideal of lawful and peaceful transitions of power all militate against successful consolidation.

In transition countries as varied in their political, economic, and cultural experiences as Russia and Indonesia, democracy's hold has been irresolute and, in some key respects, may be in retreat.

At the same time, international donors and aid organizations interested in democratization have become increasingly intent on the problem of program sustainability in the nongovernmental sectors of transition societies. This report focuses on two important elements of democratic sustainability: civil society and the media. It draws on discussion at the second International Roundtable on Journalism and Free Expression, a joint project of the Ford Foundation and the Aspen Institute, held in Santiago, Chile, March 13–16, 2001.

In its first such meeting in May 2000, Roundtable participants focused on the legal and structural obstacles that journalists face in transition societies, the ways in which journalists might view their work and their responsibilities in such situations, and the activities that nongovernmental and intergovernmental organizations could and should undertake to support free expression and a free press.

The Santiago conference took a more forward-looking view; it focused on strategies for sustaining media pluralism in the post-transition period—or, as journalist, educator, and conference moderator Geoff Cowan called them, "models that travel."

There was general agreement that any such models should serve two broad goals. The first goal is the creation and sustainability of civil society and civic values—what one participant called "enhancing the bonds of community, building citizenship, and promoting individuality." The second goal is "building a culture of free expression to which end the conferees discussed a range of issues associated with the "watchdog" role of the press and the need to provide citizens with access to news and information.

A quite different conception of the media's contribution to civil society focused on providing citizens with access to the instruments of communication, perhaps even against the prerogatives of those who own them, and especially where ownership is concentrated in the state or in private centers of economic power. These general concerns were joined in a common inquiry—how does a society create and sustain media that engage the public in democratically centered discourse?—and framed by the following specific issues:

- What are the characteristics of "civil society," and what factors affect its growth or decline? What factors make civil society a constructive agent in democratization? Can civil society be antidemocratic?
- What is the role of the state in creating and sustaining a strong civil society? What is the role of an independent and diverse press? Can a nonplural society sustain a vibrant civil society or a vibrant press system?
- What about the seemingly intractable problem of inhospitable environments—from coercive governments, antiquated press laws, and marginalized populations on the one hand to public apathy and unfavourable markets on the other? What strategies can journalists in developing societies realistically employ to circumvent, if not overcome, these obstacles to civil society and free press development?

To put some flesh on these questions, the conference opened with a lengthy examination of its host country, which emerged from bureaucratic authoritarian rule with the election of a Christian Democratic president, Patricio

Aylwin, in 1989—around the same time that much of South America returned to civilian rule after more than a decade of domination by right-wing military governments.

The modern Latin American political experience is unique in many ways, not least in the fact that the generals who ruled there did so with the aid of the U.S. government, which in the name of democracy helped launch numerous dictatorships. Officially, U.S. policy in Latin America in the years following World War II was to fight communism; in 1961 president John F. Kennedy had announced an "Alliance for Progress"—a sort of Marshall Plan for the region.

For several decades the United States provided direct military, financial, and political support as part of its Pan-American alliance against communism—particularly, in Latin America's case, against internal "enemies of freedom": labour, the poor, and the intelligentsia. Chile's experience was particularly tragic. "No other Latin American country could equal Chile's record of constitutional government," writes historian John Charles Chasteen. "For years, Chilean democracy had negotiated major ideological differences," but following the presidential victory of socialist-communist Salvadore Allende and his Popular Unity coalition in 1970—and despite the fact that Allende disavowed violent revolution in favour of constitutional process—the U.S. Central Intelligence Agency adopted a "firm and continuing policy," in the words of the agency itself, "that Allende be overthrown by a coup."

The United States embarked on an economic war against Chile, and in 1973, under General Augusto Pinochet Ugarte, the Chilean military overthrew Allende's constitutional government in what turned out to be "the bloodiest takeover in the history of Latin America." The country would not emerge from military rule until Aylwin took office in 1990, although the military—and Pinochet—have remained powerful figures in the Chilean transition, and Chileans continue to reconcile themselves with their legacy.

MEDIA AND CIVIL SOCIETY IN POST-TRANSITION SOCIETIES

The experience of Chile in the final years of the Pinochet regime illustrates the surge of civil society and media activity that precedes political transition, as well as the difficulty of sustaining that level of mobilization after the nondemocratic government has been toppled. Several Chilean hosts for the Santiago conference—among them Faride Zeran, director of the journalism school at the University of Chile—presented evidence on this point.

Speaking primarily of opposition newspapers and public affairs periodicals, Zeran said that "the independent press helped Chilean society to overcome dictatorship at the ballot box and made it possible for people to overcome their fears," but since 1989 the independent press has withered. During the decade of transition that followed the 1988 elections, Zeran said, "We did away with what Pinochet could not undo in 17 years."

Much of the independent press of which Zeran spoke had an organic relationship with political parties that were illegal under the Pinochet government. As such it also was an elite press, its audience limited to the upper strata of Chilean society. Without question those media were important incubators of dissent and principled opposition to the military regime, but most students of the Chilean transition point to television, the country's only true mass medium, as the more critical element in Pinochet's electoral defeat.

Ironically, television's rise to prominence was the result, at least in part, of Pinochet's efforts to modernize the country's communications system, place it in private hands, and orient it toward the market and away from a politically focused print press that depended heavily on the state. One consequence of that modernization was a sixfold increase in television set ownership between 1970 and 1983; television penetration had reached 95 percent at the time of the 1988 plebiscite.

That geographic and demographic reach, more than the editorial content, made television singularly important to democratic transition. Until 1988 Chilean television had offered no political debate; broadcast news under the Pinochet regime was whatever the regime said it was and typically showed political opponents only in a judicial context, where they were portrayed as criminals. Editorially independent broadcasting had ceased following the 1973 coup, when radio stations, magazines, and newspapers belonging to Unidad Popular, the left-wing coalition that had supported Allende, had been confiscated and either held by the military government or sold to private firms.

Media belonging to other parties, such as the Christian Democrats, were not officially closed but were hounded out of existence. The state television network, TVN, and all other television broadcasters came under the control of Pinochet-appointed university presidents. Within a few years, the military government ended the practice of providing public financing to television, and in 1977 it ended all restrictions on television advertising, thereby creating a unique and curious situation in which state-controlled channels were financed by the private sector.

This state of affairs began to change in 1987 with the visit of Pope John Paul II—the first-ever papal visit to the overwhelmingly Catholic country. Although the government tried to orchestrate television coverage of the visit in its favour, it was hard-put to deny or suppress the pope's public call for a return to Chile's democratic traditions. "The result," writes one commentator, "was to legitimate an ethos antagonistic to the authoritarian regime, an ethos that would eventually serve as the basis for the victory of the 'No' side in the 1988 plebiscite."

In advance of the plebiscite, under the rules of the government's National Television Council, the opposition received 15 minutes of airtime each day, although it was otherwise banned from news and public affairs programs. The opposition's brief message was juxtaposed with the government's own 15-minute message in 30-minute programs that aired between 10:45 p.m. and 11:15 p.m. on weekdays and between noon and 12:30 p.m. on weekends—time slots the government had chosen to ensure the smallest possible audience.

To the government's great chagrin, the program drew enormous audiences and became the topic of public discussion throughout the country, allowing the opposition to surmount the enormous obstacles to defeating Pinochet at the ballot box. It had to overcome the negative images that the regime had used to portray it as inefficient and violent, even as it offered no candidate or program of its own; it had to convince people cowed by 15 years of state terror that a "No" vote against the government would not result in reprisals; and it had to explain that even if Pinochet lost the plebiscite he would remain in power for a full year before there would be a presidential election.

To meet these challenges, the opposition turned over its media campaign almost entirely to a team of producers, advertising executives, reporters, and political scientists who chose to attack Pinochet with the modern techniques of democratic campaigning: focus groups and polls designed to ascertain voters' concerns, as well as public relations strategies for targeting undecided voters, especially women and the young. Instead of trying to counter the government's relentless negativity and scare tactics, the opposition chose the motto "We are more" and was positive and issue-focused.

Rather than devote its entire 15-minute broadcasts to single topics, it did short vignettes on issues ranging from poverty and health to exile and torture, all hosted by a well-known personality and featuring musical jingles, comic sketches, and the personal testimony of common citizens. Pinochet became a target of humor intended to dispel his image of political invincibility; painful subjects such as the "disappeared" were treated respectfully, as the basis for national reconciliation rather than division.

So successful was the television campaign that it became a news story in its own right, covered by the nation's print media. Importantly, where the opposition's television campaign had made the conscious decision not to respond to the government's attacks, the print media covering the campaign *did* respond, disputing the government's arguments and thus providing a valuable complement to the television campaign. This activity underscored the fact that although the television campaign was critical to political mobilization, the print media performed the essential task of providing information.

In that role, the print media were among the associations that laid the groundwork for mobilization in the realm of civil society, contributing to and interacting with the social organizations and the political opposition that Pinochet had tried to eradicate, then ignored, and finally misjudged. The television campaign reinforced activity that went on in communities and in face-to-face contact with voters.

POST TRANSITION ERA

With few exceptions, said Zeran, the dynamism that existed among the media in the years immediately before and after the plebiscite is now gone. Among the principal alternative weeklies that promoted democratization were *Cauce, Analisis,* and *APSI*—all now defunct. Much of the opposition press had relied on grants from foundations and political parties for a significant portion of its financing; when those sources dried up, circulation and advertising revenue did not suffice to pay the bills. For a time, some print media that campaigned for democracy did successfully appeal to broader and more diverse audiences, but they too have closed. The last of the important opposition weeklies, *Hoy,* closed for financial reasons in 1998, as did the independent daily *La Epoca,* which had been founded in 1987 and was generally credited for high-quality reporting leading up to the election.

La Epoca was unable to service its debt from sales and unable to attract advertisers after the transition because of advertiser discomfort with the paper's editorial view. Today Chile's newspaper market is dominated by two large and conservative conglomerates: El Mercurio, S.A., publisher of the Santiago daily *El Mercurio,* and Consorcio Periodistico, S.A. (COPESA), whose flagship paper is *La Tercera.* Both organizations gave and received financial support from the former military government. Television—which in Chile, as throughout Latin America, came of age in a period dominated by military governments—has increased its standing as the nation's principal mass medium.

TVN is now self-financing and subject to the same ratings pressures as other private broadcasters and cable channels. At the same time, TVN is subject to government oversight and interference, just as all media are subject to prosecution under the country's media laws—most notably the "contempt of authority" provisions in the criminal code, the state security law, and the code of military justice.

All of these provisions allow public officials, including judges and military officers, to bring criminal charges against news organizations for virtually any kind of criticism. Indeed, only a few weeks before the conference, a Santiago business reporter had been prosecuted under the state security law for an article that was critical of a senator—an offense that on conviction carries a five-year prison sentence.

Most worrisome, said Sebastian Brett of Human Rights Watch, is that Chileans don't seem to care much that their news media are so singularly conservative and uncritical, nor do they perceive their relative lack of choice in this regard or the government's punitive hostility to criticism as a threat to or limitation on their own expressive rights. "If freedom of speech is the oxygen of democracy," Brett asked, "why are there not people in the streets asking for air to breathe?

Zeran's observation confirmed a point discussed subsequently in this report—that the institutions and conditions that are necessary to civil society are not always sufficient to produce one—but it also raised some fundamental questions: What constitutes "media pluralism" in a society, and what role should governments and markets play in creating and sustaining it? A point of view that was not much in evidence at the Santiago conference but is well represented in the scholarly literature is that Chile's media *are* both modern and pluralistic. Indeed, unlike most democratizing countries, Chile did not witness any fundamental changes in its communications system after the fall of the old regime.

Instead, the process of privatization that began under Pinochet has continued under subsequent, democratic governments, most notably with the privatization of Radio National in 1994. Chilean television, at least, has also been globalized: Megavision is owned partly by the Mexican broadcasting giant Televisa, and 49 percent of the television operation of the Universidad de Chile is now owned by the

Venezuelan consortium Venevision. All of this activity has had the effect of reducing the government's involvement in the operational-aspects of communications—from the point of view of many free expression advocates, an essential task of any meaningful transition to a democratic media sector. It is not the only goal, of course. With respect to editorial matters, most of the conference's Chilean hosts said, the country's hostile press laws combined with the pressures of the market have had the undesirable effect of driving viewpoint diversity from Chile's media, although that perception clearly depends on how one defines viewpoint diversity.

The Aspen Institute conferees, for example, spent some time discussing *El Mostrador*, a new online news publication based in Santiago whose general manager, Federico Joannon, made clear that he and his partners were in business to turn a profit, not to serve as an opposition centre to the government. "We care about recovering democracy," Joannon said, "but that is not our key issue. We created the company and risked our capital in the belief that the Internet will become the fundamental medium. We are not committed to the government, the church, or the business community. We are not a refuge for alternative groups; that is legitimate, but not the crux of what we do.

We want to provide information to the majority of people—they have the right to be well informed, too—and are trying to be a watchdog on power, a viable business activity in the centre of the business world." Joannon's presentation prompted a discussion that wound throughout the conference about the structural, financial, and editorial foundations of media organizations and how well different configurations comport with the needs of civil society. Criticism of *El Mostrador*, for instance, centered on its "elite" character as an online only service and, more obliquely, on its non-oppositional approach to public affairs. Such criticism was not limited to the Roundtable. Not long after the conference, a *New York Times* editorial on Latin American media praised *El Mostrador* for being "daring and innovative" but closed with the charge that in Chile "as elsewhere in Latin America, the market has more often produced media that unquestioningly support the powerful in society, failing the public they are supposed to serve."

Charges such as these—especially when they come from large, private, and profitable Western media firms—are difficult to evaluate. Throughout developed democracies, for instance, the leading public affairs media, almost without exception, are private firms that earn the bulk of their revenues from advertising, not circulation. (Advertising and other forms of sales activity also have become an essential source of revenue for large public media organizations such as the British Broadcasting Corporation, which now derives about 20 percent of its annual revenues from its profit-seeking subsidiaries.)

More generally, although it may be true—as most of the conference's Santiago hosts argued—that Chile's media do a poor job of covering public affairs, it also is true that the low levels of political involvement and political polarization in the Chilean public are characteristic of consolidated democracies. In short, what some of the conferees viewed as public apathy and a diminished media market, others may fairly regard as measures of successful democratic transition.

Clearly there are multiple valid and important measures of media pluralism; where the state wields substantial powers of censorship and control, as in Chile, pluralism will suffer. It may be circumscribed further where major sources of news and information are controlled by non-media sectors of the economy with links to the government or large stakes in public policy.

COPESA, for example, is controlled by a group tied to Chile's banking industry—just as in the United States the NBC television network is owned by General Electric, a large defense contractor, and in Italy three television networks are owned by the country's prime minister.

With regard to the practical problems of *which* voices to sustain in a transition society and *how* to sustain them, however, the conference participants held a variety of conflicting views on the role that governments and nongovernmental organizations (NGOs) should play, on one hand, and the role of the market on the other.

For example, Edetaen Ojo, executive director of Media Rights Agenda in Lagos, talked about the concentration of media in southern Nigeria and the complete lack of media in the north; to him, the issue was essentially geographic, although he acknowledged that in other parts of the world, ethnic, religious, or political diversity might be what matters. With respect to the "how" question, Brett noted that in the early 1990s left-wing members of the Chilean legislature proposed to enforce pluralism by statute, essentially guaranteeing financial support for media that were unable to find sufficient footing in the market. The Chilean Supreme Court declared the law unconstitutional—a decision that Brett called correct. "Judges should not have that responsibility," he said, although he clearly supported the goal of the legislation. So how to get from here to there? Because so much of the conference discussion about media pluralism and sustainability was rooted in the language of civil society, it might be helpful to examine some of the literature and lessons from that sector in the years following the third wave.

CIVIL SOCIETY AND ITS PROBLEMS

The idea of civil society has its origins in the Scottish Enlightenment of the 18th century, although it received new visibility and celebrity in the years preceding the collapse of the Soviet Union when the political opposition to authoritarian governments in Central and Eastern Europe embraced the concept. Over the past decade untold aid monies and conferences have been devoted to civil society, and a large literature has bloomed on the subject.

Some of that literature is analytically helpful; much is conceptually muddy or romantic. Scholars debate the definition of the term; journalists use it to mean a variety of things (including simple civility) and have invoked it as a remedy for any number of political and professional ills. One commentator notes that "rarely has so heavy an analytic cargo been strapped on the back of so slender a conceptual beast." The scholarly literature on civil society generally agrees that the term excludes private business and "political society" but includes just about everything else that falls under the rubric of voluntary association, from churches and social clubs to organized labour and even organized crime.

As far as democratization is concerned, the point of these associations (ideally) is to articulate and advance social values and interests. Civil society can include large social movements (most notably, today, feminism, environmentalism, and human rights), political groups, and professional associations (including journalism and media organizations). In its modern form, civil society places renewed emphasis on ethnic, racial, and religious identities and includes a wide array of single-issue groups with varying commitments to pluralism and democracy. Still another, much-noted feature of modern civil society is its global character.

Tens of thousands of NGOs have become the locus of civil society activity, and in some cases—such as the negotiations leading up to the global climate accords at the

1992 Earth Summit in Rio de Janeiro—decisions taken in the civil society sector have rivalled or even superceded those taken in the political and economic sectors by sovereign states.

At the Aspen Institute Roundtable, discussion on civil society turned on a few core concerns. For some participants, the primary problem was (and presumably will remain for some time) building civil society; in some countries and regions, civil society is for one reason or another weak or nonexistent, and sometimes where it does exist it is not very pluralist—or worse, it is antidemocratic. For other participants, the problem was reinvigorating a civil society sector that in the years after democratic transition has withered.

CIVIL SOCIETY, THE STATE, AND DEMOCRATIC TRANSITION

Scholarship on democratization argues that the character and strength of civil society institutions depend above all on the type of regime that preceded the transition period. Political scientist Juan Linz, for example, has argued that the paths to democratic transition and consolidation vary according to whether the deposed regime was authoritarian, totalitarian, post-totalitarian, or sultanistic. As far as civil society is concerned, the defining characteristic of totalitarianism is the complete lack of political, economic, or social pluralism, all of which the state has tried systematically to obliterate.

Post-totalitarian regimes allow the emergence of some forms of social pluralism, but that pluralism usually is located within the regime itself—such as an opposition faction within the ruling party. Authoritarian regimes typically have civil society institutions that evolve outside the regime—in the private space of culture, art, and religiosity, as well as in the economy—and can be very strong but are not necessarily democratic in impulse.

In China, for example, the civil society sector has grown dramatically in recent years, but that growth has not been accompanied by any significant democratization movement. In sultanistic societies, Linz writes, the defining characteristic of the regime is unrestrained personal leadership of the kind that typified Marcos' Philippines, Haiti under the Duvaliers, Mobutu Sese Seko's Zaire (Congo), Suharto's Indonesia, or Iran under the Shah. In such societies, all forms of pluralism are precarious; where civil society exists, it is subject to the whims of the ruler, for whom the state and the military are personal instruments to be used at the ruler's discretion.

With each type of nondemocratic regime, Linz argues, the most important element in the development of civil society after the transition is the concurrent development of the rule of law and the guarantee of civil liberties. The corollary to this argument is important—and a subject of considerable discussion at the Santiago conference: *The most effective guarantee of a healthy civil society is a strong state, and the struggle between civil society and the state is not a zero-sum game.*

Indeed, in the absence of a strong state, civil society can easily erupt in civil war; most of the armed conflicts since the end of the Cold War have been intrastate affairs in ethnically and religiously pluralist countries where the proliferation of civil society associations devoted to narrow causes threatened or destroyed democratic transition.

In a 1998 editorial that was sharply critical of "civil society romantics," the Indian newspaper *The Hindu* observes that "civil society finds as much space for casteist, class, communal and patriarchal projects as for movements challenging all these, and dominant structures in civil society can neutralize democratic agendas." Moreover, as conference participant Bimo Nugroho said of the Indonesian experience, weak or corrupt states can politicize civil society and thus exacerbate rather than ameliorate social differences. This is as true among nations as it is within them. Several commentators have noted that the global activities of many NGOs and international governmental organizations (IGOs) have played a role in triggering ethnic nationalism and religious fundamentalism, both of which tear at the state, encourage human rights violations, and provoke humanitarian crises.

In short, civil society gains that come at the expense of a weakened state, although predictable and perhaps even healthy in the short term, may not be supportive of democratization in the long term. As political theorist Michael Walzer writes, The state itself is unlike all the other associations. It both frames civil society and occupies space within it. It fixes the boundary conditions and the basic rules of all associational activity.

It compels association members to think about a common good, beyond their own conceptions of the good life....And across the entire range of association, individual men and women need to be protected against the power of officials, employers, experts, party bosses, factory foremen, directors, priests, parents, patrons; and small and weak groups need to be protected against large and powerful ones. For civil society, left to itself, generates radically unequal power relationships which only state power can challenge.

That is not to say that civil society joined with a strong state automatically results in political pluralism. Even where governments are strong and ostensibly liberal, they are not necessarily supportive of civil society. Running roughly concurrent with the most recent global wave of democratization has been the rise in Western developed societies of what some scholars call "authoritarian liberalism"—the process by which the role of the market in social organization has been maximized and that of civil society diminished, sometimes with strong impetus from governments.

According to John Dryzek, for example, the British government under prime minister Margaret Thatcher attacked the conditions of civil society by trying to restrict the activities of trade unions, limit press freedom (including in particular that of the British Broadcasting Corporation), curtail the rights of criminal defendants, make local authorities more responsive to the central government, politicize the police, and so on.

Many authoritarian states—China, Vietnam, and Iran, to name a few—have allowed political, social, and economic liberalization to enlarge the space for civil society operations, but only because the government regards those operations as central to its own goals of control. In China, for example, privately published newspapers now far outnumber state papers and engage in investigative reporting and muckraking. Journalists have to carefully self-censor themselves, though not always. When the ruling party began its own highly publicized anticorruption campaign, it encouraged the private print press to join in.

Chinese television features live news, call-in programs, and celebrity interviews, and the government allows a great deal of general news and entertainment programming to enter the country, but the growth of electronic media is largely the result of market reforms and the government's desire to invest in growth industries, and the government does not hesitate to jam international broadcasts that are critical of the regime. Groups that represent broad portions of the population (such as women's groups) and have aims that are not clearly focused on officially stated goals typically have a harder time establishing themselves.

When they do it is often because they undertake some "acceptable" activity; the government looks favorably upon groups that give support to women living in poverty, for example, but not to those that object to the official economic policies that keep them there. Many democratization studies note that in some regions of the world—particularly Pacific Asia and the Middle East—the dividing line between the government and society is neither clear nor immutable. The Chinese language, it is said, has many terms for "state" but none for "civil society."

Nomenclature aside, many scholars argue that civil society does not really exist in Pacific Asia—at least not in the liberalizing sense in which Western political theorists use the term. The thrust of the argument focuses on an "illiberal middle class" that emphasizes "community rather than autonomy and moral certainty rather than tolerance" and has a substantial economic stake in the stability of the public sector.

One piece of evidence in this theory is the extent to which press freedom is curtailed throughout the region. Self-censorship is common; where it fails, as one commentator put it in a description of the South Korean media, the state is regularly "on hand to offer Confucian guidance."

Several of the Aspen Institute conferees described similarly illiberal civil society tendencies in their own countries or regions. In Egypt, said Basma El-Husseiny, a Ford Foundation participant at the Santiago conference, society itself is "nonplural" and thus there is fairly low tolerance among the public for diverse ideas or even free expression generally.

At present, she said, the most potent elements of Egyptian civil society are the Islamic groups that "provide educational institutions, provide services to the community, and work on conservative legislation." One measure of their effectiveness can be found in news reports that Cairo's al-Azhar University—for a millennium the unrivalled centre of higher education in the Islamic world—has embarked on a censorship campaign to weed out vice from Arabic literature, film, theater, music, and scholarship. Konstanty Gebert, consultant to the Media Development Loan Fund and a columnist for *Gazeta Wyborcza* in Warsaw, made a similar observation about the political influence of Catholic and Jewish fundamentalists in Poland and Israel, respectively.

In some countries the lines between civil society and the authority of the state simply do not exist; the government itself dominates the civil society sector through government-owned nongovernmental organizations (GONGOs). In authoritarian Iran, for example, large public-assistance organizations known as *bunyads* are linked with the ruling clergy and dominate national finance, housing, transportation, and agriculture.

In many Middle Eastern societies, there are so-called Royal NGOs whose boards of directors are appointed by royal decree; these Royal NGOs carry out government development projects. There also are many independent NGOs that are not registered with the government and thus are technically illegal (as in Kuwait); they manage to survive, however, in part because they enjoy support from key parliamentary committees.

CIVIL SOCIETY AFTER THE TRANSITION

For many Santiago conference participants, the problem with civil society is how to sustain it in something other than a purely oppositional form after the early period of democratic transition. Several scholarly and political commentators looking at transition societies from Central

Europe to Latin American have commented on the processes of civil society takeoff, stagnation, and institutionalization—in short, the gradual inclusion of civil society into the state after transition and the consequent weakening of the civil society sector.

One commentator describes these processes as "demobilization" and decapitation. "Demobilization occurs when democratic transition follows a negotiated settlement between the old regime and civil society. This is precisely what happened in most of Eastern and Central Europe in 1989–1990, where national roundtable negotiations were critical to transitions in Poland, Hungary, Czechoslovakia, and East Germany.

In the course of negotiations, some of the enmity that exists between the state and civil society softens, and in any event the immediate reason for civil society's intensity—exclusion from political life—disappears. Very often demobilization is a conscious decision, taken to make way for the development of democratic politics.

In Chile, for example, much of the civil society movement in fact was the creation of the outlawed Christian Democrat and Socialist parties. In the period after the 1988 plebiscite, these parties were again able to participate legally in politics and consciously chose to demobilize so that they could get on with the business of governing.

Decapitation occurs when many of civil society's most articulate and active spokespeople are drawn into the new government, as in Poland and the Czech Republic, thereby depriving civil society organizations of their leadership. The irony is that decapitation is most likely where civil society has been most successful in promoting democratization. In some transition societies, demobilization and decapitation are particularly troublesome because civil society is weak to begin with. In post-communist European states, even those that liberalized in the years following Stalin's death in 1950, many civil society organizations had little opportunity to escape state serutiny and harassment or to engage in autonomous social action.

So long was the experience of repression that civil society organizations were simply crushed out of existence—and, as important, out of memory. In Latin America, by contrast, the bureaucratic authoritarian regimes that ruled virtually the entire region in 1970 also were relatively short-lived; following democratic transition about a decade ago, political parties, trade unions, and other repressed organizations were resurrected, often with the same leadership that existed before dictatorship.

More generally, most Latin American countries had had experience with the political and institutional elements that are essential to civil society: an accountable executive, a capable bureaucracy, laudatory experience with civil and political rights, the rule of law, and transparency in political decision making.

In Central and Eastern Europe, civil society has been further strained by economic reforms that, though necessary, have effectively created dual societies—one far better off than the other economically and socially. Dual societies commonly exist in other developed and developing countries, but in Central and Eastern Europe the duality is particularly divisive because so many of the old structures of socialist production now coexist with large sectors of the economy that have adapted to the competitive market. Latin America again provides an interesting contrast.

By the time Pinochet stepped down in 1989, for example, Chile had the strongest economy in the region, one that enjoyed broad popular support. All of the Christian Democratic presidents that followed the dictator—Patricio Aylwin, Eduardo Frei, and now Socialist Ricardo Lagos—

have emphasized social justice, but none has introduced significant economic changes.

Arguably, the economic stability that Pinochet brought to Chile also has provided some of the necessary social stability for the continuing investigation of and national reckoning with the dictator's crimes. Not all of these factors (e.g., demobilization and decapitation) argue against the creation of civil society, and some are short-term problems.

New leaders eventually will replace old ones, for instance. Other problems are more serious. By its nature, civil society is about the creation of social unity through fragmentation and conflict; in dual societies, however, such conflict is apt to have less to do with governance than with the allocation of state resources. Where governments are weak, this kind of civil society discord can be antidemocratic and destabilizing.

CIVIL SOCIETY AND MEDIA PLURALISM

In an important background paper prepared for the Santiago conference, legal scholar Monroe Price defines media sustainability in terms of "reasonable objectives" and whether sufficient and varied revenues exist to meet them. Some objectives may be perfectly reasonable (maximizing audiences, for example) but make little or no contribution to the information needs (balanced and complete reporting, presentation and discussion of opposing political views) of healthy civil society association.

The choice of objectives is critical: Because news and public affairs reporting may cost more to produce than other kinds of content and, at the least, competes for time or space that otherwise could go to more lucrative fare (e.g., entertainment), a newspaper or television station that provides news and information may find that the *level* of revenues necessary for sustainability is higher, as well as that the *sources* of those revenues are fewer or significantly different (for instance, not-for-profit rather than for-profit). Thus, although sustaining a variety of media may be important as a general civil society goal ("the key to civic engagement," according to one conference participant), it matters a lot what *particular* civil society goals a country's media policy is supposed to serve.

At the Santiago conference, for instance, it was not always clear what goals participants had in mind when they spoke of "media pluralism." In economic terms, for example, pluralism might be measured in terms of *product* diversity (the number of media choices available to consumers); in normative terms it might be measured in *idea* diversity (point-of-view variation, which presumably is essential to rich democratic discourse) or *access* diversity (a variant on idea diversity that seeks to make sure all ideas get adequate time and emphasis).

In practice, pluralism is likely to be a function of some combination of these measures. Talking about media coverage of the second *Intifada*, for example, Daoud Kuttab of the Institute of Modern Media at Al-Quds University in Ramallah spoke about the development of Arab satellite stations, local television, and radio and their importance in how the world—and especially Arabs themselves—viewed the Palestinian-Israeli conflict.

Whereas the major wire services often were biased and Arab state television tightly controlled, Kuttab said, satellite stations allowed people to see "professional Arab journalists working for the BBC or other western agencies reporting on how the conflict was affecting the Palestinians, and also giving time to Israeli officials who speak Arabic." At the community level, he said, local stations had the "unique opportunity to literally stick their cameras out the window, sit under the table, and give the audience an amazing show." Thus, many Arab television audiences had both product and idea diversity: more channels to choose from and perspectives other than the government's.

At some point, however, the logic of markets suggests that increasing competition will drive overall quality down rather than up. The result is a media system that has product diversity (arguably an important civil society requirement) but provides little of the news and information the democratization needs (idea diversity) and where consumers may reduce rather than increase their consumption of information (thus diminishing access diversity). Even as Kuttab lauded the variety of choices now available to Arab viewers, for instance, he bemoaned the fact that the private stations depend on advertising and the public stations become "government mouthpieces."

"There is little room between these two choices," he said, "and only international funding keeps alive a third way." There is an important civil society and media sustainability issue here: Programming subsidies, whatever their source, may have little or no practical effect because increasing the amount and variety of information does not change the fact that the fundamental market failure is at the point of consumption, not supply.

That is not to say that satisfying consumer values should be the primary concern of a media system or that non-quantifiable social values do not matter—only that the values that *are* emphasized in a media system will have consequences that play out in the realm of civil society and media sustainability.

Some conference participants were less concerned with access diversity, for example, than they were with public access to the instruments of mass communication. Such a concern shifts the emphasis in values from free expression to open communication—from the rights of speakers to the rights of audiences; it also may suggest that the media's free press rights are to be balanced against the public's free speech rights and that the government has a role in balancing the two.

Finally, the issue of media sustainability has to be considered at the micro level, in terms of the *particular* goals a media organization serves. Different goals come with different expectations about sustainability. Bosnia-Herzegovina, for example, is home to more than 270 radio and television stations, many of them supported by NGOs and IGOs. Some were created to provide information during the crisis of war and reconstruction, others to facilitate democratic transition, and still others to counter nationalist programming from Zagreb and Belgrade.

At some future date, many of these stations will close after they lose the benefit of donor assistance, and presumably many should as the country stabilizes. Among the media that remain, some will feature mostly low-quality entertainment fare and sensationalism.

The problem of sustaining these media, Price notes, is less interesting, and arguably less important, than sustaining "more public-oriented stations"—including, perhaps, even state-supported stations that compete with them. Where these sustainability issues get truly difficult are where the goals of "independent" media are ambiguous (like independence itself).

Recently, for example, the Russian company Media-MOST lost control over its television station NTV and its publishing house *Sem Dnej* (Seven Days, publisher of the daily *Segodnya* and the weekly newsmagazine *Itogi*) to the huge and partly state-owned gas utility Gazprom, which technically controls only 46 percent of Media-Most but called in $300 million worth of loans in 2000 and staged an armed raid on the station on April 15, 2001.

In the weeks before the raid, American media mogul Ted Turner and financier George Soros reportedly offered to buy approximately 19 percent of NTV's shares from Vladimir Gusinsky for $225 million; the Russian Duma firmly rejected a resolution to support the station; and on March 31 between 10,000 to 20,000 Muscovites rallied in Pushkin Square holding signs that read, "We want our NTV."

After the raid, more than 350 NTV employees reportedly quit or were fired, some going over to Gusinsky's cable channel TNT, which reaches only about half of Russia's 145 million people and also is deeply in debt to Gazprom.

At one point several of NTV's journalists tried to negotiate a merger with another independent channel—Boris Berezovsky's TV-6—but no deal ever materialized. Eduard Sagalaev, the respected journalist who had led TV-6, was replaced in March by Igor Shabdurasulov, a former government official, and Berezovsky himself has fled the country to avoid criminal charges.

International observers have rightfully condemned the "Kremlin's determination to reassert its dominance over the news media," but much of the criticism overlooks the fact that neither Gusinsky nor Berezovsky was a model of professional independence or integrity.

During the Yeltsin years, NTV had been alternatively opposed to the government's policies and openly allied with them, and Berezovsky reportedly gained the chairmanship of his media empire by having the previous chairman assassinated. Yet NTV had done some distinguished and critical reporting, making its reputation for independence in its coverage of the Chechen wars, and both NTV and TV-6 were free of the large banking, mining, oil, and electricity conglomerates, many of them state-owned, that control most of Russia's other major media outlets.

The issues of government interference at NTV played out in dramatic fashion but have not been unique to Russia. Similar conflicts have occurred in Poland, Hungary, Slovakia, Romania, Bulgaria, and the Czech Republic, in each case with government broadcasting councils dominated by the ruling party making top editorial appointments to national television or radio stations.

Unlike their Western European counterparts, public broadcasters in Central and Eastern Europe typically lack the layers of administrative insulation necessary to ensure editorial independence. Nor is it unusual for journalists at public stations to maintain close contact with government officials, particularly those who appointed them, or for politicians to telephone editors in advance of an election to complain that coverage of their parties is unfair or inadequate.

Journalists in the region have responded to these pressures in a variety of ways and with mixed results. In Slovenia, for example, public broadcasters in 1999 published an extensive code of professional ethics, in the process staking out the boundaries that define editorial independence from state and private sources of influence and interference. As impressive as the code is, it doubtlessly is more effective because Slovenian public broadcasters enjoy a source of revenue (surcharges on viewers' electricity bills) that is independent of the state budget and because the country's broadcast council is not appointed by the parliament.

Czech public media also earn revenues from a license fee, but the independence of Czech Television came under international scrutiny in late 2000 and early 2001 when the government council that oversees the station dismissed its director and replaced him with Jiri Hodac, an experienced former BBC editor who purportedly had connections with former prime minister Vaclav Klaus and his Civic Democratic

Party. The journalists at Czech Television suspected government meddling and had their suspicions confirmed when Hodac named former journalist and Klaus economic advisor Jana Bobosikova as the station's news director.

She promptly fired several editors and staffers, at which point the editors barricaded themselves in the newsroom and for a period of weeks broadcast their own "unofficial" version of the news, using satellite and cable links. President Vaclav Havel and other prominent Czech writers and artists gave support to the protestors, and at one point some 75,000 Czechs rallied to their cause in Wencelas Square, turning the entire episode into an international embarrassment for the government. Hodac eventually resigned and his cadre of new managers was fired; all of the protesting editors stayed on, including those whom Bobosikova had fired weeks earlier. Presumably the outcome of the Czech Television seizure was a victory for press independence—that was the common consensus in news accounts everywhere—but another view, carefully articulated at the Santiago conference by Jeremy Druker, editor of *Transitions Online* in Prague, was that the rebels (as they called themselves) may have paid a bit too dearly for their cause.

"The journalists behind the protests did a great job of manipulating their own media," Druker said, "and were not at all independent or objective in their coverage of their own demonstration." Ironically, Hodac had argued before resigning that one of his goals was to make Czech Television more professional. He also, had said he wanted to make the service more efficient in the face of increased competition and a continually dwindling audience share.

STRATEGIES FOR MEDIA SUSTAINABILITY

The Russian and Czech experiences, no less than Chile's or any number of others, raise several questions about the matrix of media sustainability and, as Monroe Price calls it, the "ideal form of sustainability." For a brief time at the Roundtable -there was discussion on this subject in terms of the optimal mix of not-for-profit and for profit private media, public and private sources of revenue. That discussion ranged broadly between the "BBC model" of social democratic journalism with its direct state subsidies and the "American" model of liberal journalism, with its reliance on the market and indirect state subsidies (through the tax code, antitrust law, postal regulations, and so on).

The participants soon agreed, however, that this subject was treated extensively elsewhere (including, notably, in other Aspen Institute publications) and probably was of limited relevance to the experience of transition societies. Eventually, they gave detailed attention to three strategies for promoting media pluralism that most believed were economically sustainable and supportive of the democratizing features of civil society.

- *Build coalitions between media organizations and NGOs.* In some cases this might mean actually developing media capacity for an NGO so that it makes an independent contribution to the mix of media in a society; it also could mean providing media outlets with programming on important public issues or educating journalists and media organizations about the role they play, for better or worse, in civil society development. Several conference participants, for instance, encouraged media literacy programs (for the general public and for journalists, who often know too little about the effects of their work) and various forms of media criticism (e.g., program monitoring, academic studies, ombudsmen).
- *Develop unconventional uses of traditional media and experiment with new media to reach underserved*

or marginalized populations and promote civil society development in ways that mainstream media may not or cannot. Video and audio recordings on tape or CD-ROM are relatively inexpensive and allow easy distribution of programming. Entertainment and other non-news media—television soap operas, videogames or novellas, even public relations campaigns—can be as effective as news and public affairs programming, maybe more so, in promoting democratic values. The Internet, of course, can open access to people who are not professional communicators and allow them to take part in shaping civil society and the practice of journalism.

- *Learn and apply the basics of management—economics, financial accounting, and marketing—and use them to secure loans and other sources of capital.* A clear subtext of the Santiago conference was that journalism organizations in post-transition societies, whether for-profit or not-for-profit, cannot ignore the demands and opportunities of the market. In this regard, developing and sustaining the core business is only part of the challenge.

With some variation, these strategies are the same as those taught in media seminars at leading management schools—which typically emphasize the need to articulate clear organizational values and then make them operational through joint ventures, experiments and learning projects, and a more sophisticated understanding of audiences and their needs. The virtue of these strategies—indeed, what makes them effective—is that they are mutually reinforcing. Three case studies at the Santiago conference illustrated how they might work; interestingly, one had its origins in the women's movement, another in advertising, and the third in journalism; two were not-for-profit, the other for-profit.

Radio Journal Perempuan, Indonesia

In the tumultuous transition period that followed the fall of Suharto in 1988, the number of Indonesians living in poverty has increased from 20 million to 80 million, said Gadis Arivia, chief editor of *Jurnal Perempuan (Women's Journal)*, and the impact of the change has been felt most acutely by women and children. Unemployment among women is high; the price of contraception, which was once affordable, has jumped substantially even as incomes have fallen; anemia among pregnant women as well as maternal and infant mortality have significantly increased. So too have domestic violence, rape, and sexual harassment. Saying "democracy without women is not a democracy," Arivia described her organization as an NGO engaged in nonpartisan "committed journalism" that sought to demand access for women to decision making in the public and private sectors and to encourage "positive representation" of women in the mainstream media. *Jurnal Perempuan*, which has received grants from the United States

Agency for International Development (USAID) and the Royal Dutch Embassy, is a 5,000-circulation journal read mostly by academics and professionals. More interesting, at least in the context of the Santiago conference, are the organization's other activities. One is training academics and journalists to be more aware of gender issues in their teaching and reporting. That effort includes advocating for women journalists, who make up 30–40 percent of the reporting corps in Indonesia but rarely get the best assignments and almost never break into management.

A second activity is *Radio Jurnal Perempuan* (*RJP*), a 20-minute weekly radio program for women that airs on more than 100 stations across the country's thousands of islands. The program is distributed on audiotape and now on CD-ROM and, according to Arivia, is heard by 5 million to 6 million women every week. Actually getting the program on the air, however, was not easy. The men who make the programming decisions at radio stations did not care much for *RJP's* content or its audience demographic, so "we paid for the first three months to get radio stations to put Indonesian women on the air," Arivia said.

Even now, some stations cut stories from the program that they don't like. As the program found its audience, "we bargained again and got the price down, and now we don't pay at all. Now we ask our station partners to contribute, and about 60 percent do. We try to attract sponsors, and many are interested, but they are not always the sponsors we like. We have The Body Shop, which is excellent. Philip Morris is very keen to advertise, and the money is tempting, but it's Philip Morris. Nestle wants more passive and domesticated women than what we cover."

REGIONAL REACH LIMITED, KENYA

A second case study focused on providing video programming to the large rural populations in Africa who are out of reach of virtually all media except state radio. With cooperation from the government (which provides security), the for-profit organization Regional Reach Ltd. in Nairobi provides free televisions and videocassette recorders (VCRs) to rural communities, placing them in central village locations. People then congregate to watch entertainment and news programs that Regional Reach provides on VHS tapes, said Rose Kimotho, a former advertising executive who founded and now directs the service.

A typical tape starts with the state television program, Kimotho said, but then moves on to subjects such as farming, AIDS, football, music, and religion. Revenue for the service comes from advertising, but some programming is provided through partnerships with not-for-profit organizations—churches, for example, and USAID, which paid for 40 television sets and VCRs in return for free distribution of its messages on AIDS and malaria.

The service operates in 200 village centers and has about 1 million adult viewers each month; as Regional Reach moves from VHS tapes to terrestrial broadcast transmission, Kimotho said, those numbers will increase.

> *"For many of these people," she said, "it's the first time they've ever seen a TV. It's like being in a theater—it's very quiet. There are many runners from our area who so far as anyone remembers just left the village and went somewhere else. So we have programs on athletics, and they see these people running in Europe, in colour and on TV. The impact is amazing—it's the first contact they have with the wider world. Until now it was just government news on the radio."*

Media Development Loan Fund, Czech Republic and United States

No one at the Santiago conference spoke more directly to its topic—or the participants' concerns—than Konstanty Gebert, a writer for *Gazeta Wyborcza* and former vice president for the Media Development Loan Fund (MDLF), which has offices in Prague and New York. Saying that grants "are fine under dictatorship and transition," Gebert objected that they also are short-lived, tied to the goals of the grantor, and "corrupting—both literally, and in the sense that they make us comfortable with not being accountable to financial money." On that conviction, he and several colleagues created MDLF in 1996 to promote editorially independent and financially self-sustaining media in developing democracies.

A private foundation, MDLF is a not-for-profit, "mission-oriented" venture capital fund that provides low-interest loans and other forms of financing to media firms in Central and Eastern Europe, Russia, Asia, Africa, and Latin America; MDLF's own list of donors and lenders includes government agencies (e.g., from the Netherlands, Switzerland, and Sweden) and NGOs (e.g., the Open Society Institute and the MacArthur Foundation).

Importantly, with its loans MDLF also provides management training and assistance. "We want our money back," said Gebert. "We behave like a major investment bank, and one element of the loan contract is that on the management and business side we rule. We never interfere with editorial policies—editorial assistance is purely voluntary, technological assistance on the same basis—but the demands on the business side have to be executed. Our clients wind up improved journalistically, but also with business expertise that makes it possible for them to compete."

Since its founding, MDLF has disbursed $15 million in loans, of which borrowers have so-far repaid $3 million in principal and interest. No loans go to state media or to media with foreign ownership. "The whole idea is that it is possible to be independent and make a profit and not be killed by the loan," Gebert said.

As discussion at the Roundtable made clear, MDLF's approach to media sustainability is unfamiliar and even vaguely threatening to news organizations that still identify with the alternative role they played in the period prior to and immediately following democratic transition. (It is a safe bet that MDLF's approach also would appear unfamiliar and threatening to many media organizations in stable industrialized democracies, many of which have only recently begun to think seriously about strategy and do not face the obstacles—well-financed, competitive state media; little or no access to capital; restrictive press laws—that media in democratizing countries typically do.) According to Gebert, fewer than half of the media organizations that have sought MDLF's help have received loans. After working through the business plan with MDLF managers, some have decided not to take the loan.

CONCLUSION

Each of the foregoing examples draws on at least two of the sustainability strategies identified at the Santiago conference. Each suggests ways of thinking about media contributions to democratization that are conceptually and operationally different from the oppositional, crisis-driven, and donor-supported models that accompanied democratic transition and its immediate aftermath. Certainly in many cases—in the Balkans, for instance—sustainability can still be measured primarily by political objective: the need to provide information in an election, to incubate independent and professional media where there are none, or even to provide opposition or clandestine media in opposition to antidemocratic regimes.

In societies in which democratic consolidation is under way, however, the problems of media sustainability mirror those of civil society and probably require similar responses: new and more varied kinds of civic and professional associations, perhaps less overtly partisan, that speak to a broader array of social needs and aspirations.

That said, the sustainability strategies discussed at the Santiago Roundtable raise issues that require further consideration from journalists and NGOs, scholars and policymakers. The first issue concerns journalism's relationship to civil society and what kinds of journalism best suit the needs of post-transition democratizing societies.

RJP's strategy of building a coalition of other NGOs, government funders, and private advertisers around the women's movement, for example, prompted a short discussion about whether such activity is an appropriate journalistic exercise or one that compromises (or at least risks) editorial independence. On the whole, the conference participants were enthusiastic about "developing models that bring civil society together with the press and force journalists to see themselves as part of a larger society, not just a club," as one described the process. Several conferees spoke favorably of "public journalism" (sometimes also called "civic" or "participatory" journalism), which some media scholars have suggested might have particular value in democratizing societies.

Although many of these associations clearly are valuable, as with civil society associations generally there is nothing inherently democratic or even "civil" about coalitions of media organizations, private firms, and NGOs—none of which can be called to account at the ballot box. Moreover, where such coalitions do serve civil society goals, sustaining them may not be so easy.

An issue that was central to the Roundtable topic but little discussed was whether *Radio Jurnal Perempuan* or any similarly popular news and public affairs medium could long survive its own success. Jeremy Druker of *Transitions Online* (itself a relatively new provider of high-quality news and information in Central and Eastern Europe) pointedly asked Arivia Gadis, for example, whether *RJP* might one day find itself "shut out" of the women's programming market as commercial stations realized that market's value and began to offer duplicative—if less sensitive or valuable—programming.

The implication of the question is critical: Even if *RJP* remains a not-for-profit, high-quality service with no direct competition, other entrants in the women's programming market will increase the competition for audiences and revenues and thus deprive *RJP* of the flexibility it now enjoys in soliciting private and public support—a loss that inevitably will have consequences for its-mission and its programming. In short, as the Ford Foundation's Jon Funabiki suggested, the forces that transform civil society associations in the period after democratic transition have their corollaries in the media sector.

Their effect *may* be detrimental to media pluralism, and thus to civil society, but not necessarily. Again, much depends on what one values in a media system and what the system's goals are. In the post-transition phase, several conference participants said, consumer commercial media that are not especially political or sophisticated—soap operas, novellas, video games, advertising—also can be the most effective in addressing broad social needs such as literacy and family planning.

A final issue of importance to civil society development is the continued advance of telecommunications that allow reciprocal exchange of news and information and, as important, the means for ordinary citizens to join in and change journalistic practice. Despite the presence of two important Internet news organizations at the Santiago conference—*El Mostrador* and *Transitions Online*—Internet communications did not receive much attention there. Presumably, the omission owed in part to the relative lack of access that citizens in many transition countries have even to basic telecommunications; fixed-line telephone density in Africa, for example, is between 1 and 2 per 10,000 people, and according to the United Nations fewer than 1 percent of Africans have access to the Internet.

Deployment of new technologies, from wireless telephony to satellites, will increase global access rates, and several thoughtful commentators have argued that as Internet use grows it will restructure power in a populist direction by politicizing mass audiences and making elites and political and economic intermediaries less important. Internet communications can be effective in circumventing state repression or, at the least, pushing it into the glare of the international spotlight.

In Zimbabwe, for example, the cellular company Ecoweb functions as an Internet service provider—effectively breaking the telecommunication monopoly held by the government—and features headlines from the *Zimbabwe Standard* and the *Zimbabwe Independent*, two independent newspapers that have been targets of government harassment. In Russia, *Itogi*, the popular newsmagazine lost in the Gazprom takeover of Media-MOST, now publishes its "official" version on the Internet, calling the company's version a "fabrication."

The counter-argument to these developments, and to the predictions for democratization that follow them, holds that in the United States and in Western European democracies—where Internet use is highest and electronic information is widely available—there has not been a corresponding increase in political engagement. Although Internet communication may make political systems more fluid and accessible, one commentator writes, the long-term result may be pluralism of a more "fragmented and unstable character."

Journalists in some transition countries—Russia, for example—already have witnessed the rise of antidemocratic online communications; as Internet communication becomes more ubiquitous, it will change the contours of discussion about civil society and the media.

In the end, what may be most helpful to the sustainability discussion is a clearer statement of the values at stake in democratization and the operational measures by which a healthy civil society and a pluralistic media system are to be judged. Journalists must remember that they can aid in reporting and analysis, but they cannot always chart the course of democratic consolidation—and should not be expected to.

Walter Lippmann once wrote that "the problem of the press is confused because the critics and the apologists expect the press to...make up for all that was not foreseen in the theory of democracy." The Santiago Roundtable on Freedom of Expression made some significant strides toward sorting out the confusion, but as the third wave settles—as some democracies consolidate and others lapse—the interplay of journalism, civil society, and democratization will warrant continued close attention.

7

POLITICAL JOURNALISM AND DEMOCRACY

INTRODUCTION

The post-Cold War period has presented an opportunity unmatched since the end of World War II to restructure the media systems of much of the world. Free of political repression or ideological constraint, media in developing and developed nations have had the opportunity to ask: Consistent with democratic principles, what should a media system look like? And more specifically for countries emerging from authoritarian rule, what news media practices promote democratization?

The Aspen Institute Communications and Society Program, in partnership with the Ford Foundation, convened the first Aspen Institute International Roundtable on Journalism, "Principles and Practice of a Free and Responsible Press: Lessons from Societies in Conflict and Transition," at the Wye River Conference Centre in late spring 2000 to examine the conditions necessary for developing and sustaining vigorous and professional journalism practice in emerging democracies.

More nations than ever before are nominally democratic, though many still labour under legal, economic, and political obstacles extant from more repressive regimes, and everywhere cultural factors-among them religion, race, and ethnicity-affect the pace and process of democratization. In some regions-the Balkans, Central and Western Africa, Indonesia, to name the most obvious-these social and cultural legacies have led to violent conflict. As with the post-war period, some media restructuring over the last decade has been the result of international military intervention, for example in Bosnia-Herzegovina and more recently in Kosovo. The difference between the current period and the post-war period, however, is the greater involvement today of intergovernmental organizations (IGOs) such as, in the Balkan case, the Organization for Security and Cooperation in Europe (OSCE) and the North Atlantic Treaty Organization (NATO), and nongovernmental organizations (NGOs), of which some 1,600 are registered with the United Nations.

Law professor Monroe Price, a participant at the conference, has observed that the international community generally takes one of two approaches to media development.* One has been essentially a topdown approach, to create under IGO control alternative sources of information that are in structure and in content, "neutral and peaceoriented."

The other is a bottom-up approach, more commonly used by NGOs, that focuses on "strengthening local, indigenous media outlets, particularly those that strike a new voice, in the hopes of building a public sphere, a civil society, and the long-term machinery for peace and reconstruction."

The Aspen Institute conferees-most of them journalists from developing nations in Africa, Asia, Central and Eastern Europe, and Latin America-were generally critical of such democratization and media development efforts by NGOs and IGOs, faulting the efforts for being too often culturally inappropriate or, for various reasons, ineffective or unsustainable. Sometimes they are simply counter productive. The topdown approach-to media development, Price observed, is apt to alienate locals, including journalists, who see it as foreign, offensive, or even hostile to their interests.

Moreover, where the approach succeeds it may do so at the cost of weakening indigenous media that cannot compete with a heavily subsidized, well-equipped news organization. If that organization later collapses when international support is withdrawn, the net effect of intervention may be a media system as weak or weaker than existed at the point of intervention. The bottom-up approach to intervention, on the other hand, must by design find its way through a media environment where, particularly in post-conflict societies, media organizations are likely to be partisan rather than independent, and reporting standards are often low or in decline.

Given the limitations to these two approaches, Price said, perhaps the international community should step back and ask itself a few questions:

What factors constitute a basis for international intervention in another nation's media system? What interventions are necessary or desirable? What are the limitations of intervention? In response to these *Professor Price, Danciger Professor of Law at the Benjamin Cardozo School of Law of Yeshiva University, submitted an excellent background paper on these subjects. See Monroe E. Price, ed., Restructuring the Media in Post-Conflict Societies: Four Perspectives, the Experience of Intergovernmental and Non-Governmental Organizations. University of Oxford: Programme in Comparative Media Law & Policy, Centre for Socio-Legal Studies, May 2000, questions, the conferees' concerns fell broadly into four areas.

They agreed that positive results could occur by:

- Promoting governmental reform, in particular reform of constitutional and statutory restrictions on journalism and the development of a strong, independent judiciary system supportive of expressive rights;
- Developing professionalism among journalists and in news organizations through the creation of external mechanisms (such as journalists' associations) and internal ones (such as ombudsmen) that set and enforce standards of practice, and through developing training programs for journalists, particularly in ethics but also in specialized substantive areas of importance to regional and local audiences;
- Supporting the development of civil society; and
- Promoting the development of a sustainable communications infrastructure.

Two important subtexts wove through the discussion on these four areas, and they provide the context around which this narrative is organized. The first concerned the role of free expression in a civil society; the second concerned the relationship between journalism and democracy in the age of economic and information globalism.

FREE EXPRESSION IN A CIVIL SOCIETY

In many emerging democracies, media law and a culture supportive of free expression are works in progress, dependent on enabling political, social, and economic conditions that, if they exist, are fragile. Throughout the developing world, for instance, government restrictions on the press commonly come in the form of litigation for offenses such as criminal, blasphemous, and civil libel, and violations of national security or emergency regulations.

Generally, licensing requirements for journalists and severe restrictions on access to government information still characterize many developing societies. Several conference participants complained of "antiquated" press laws and inadequate constitutions that enable governments to regulate expression through the power of the raised eyebrow-or, should they choose, prosecution or brute force.

Such antiquities are common even in media systems of developed countries, and are usually rooted in the experience of some earlier political regime or technological era. Israel's defense regulations, for example, were imposed during British rule in Palestine and incorporated into Israeli law after independence. The regulations allow official censorship and the detention of journalists, and Israel uses them to control coverage of military affairs.

The issue, ultimately, is not whether archaic laws and regulations exist but how they are used. Britain, for example, is a fairly benign country with respect to press rights, and its media are among the most vibrant in the world. British press law, however, is restrictive, and there exist no fewer than forty-eight nations in the world, many of them former colonies in Africa, Asia, and the Middle East, where both the legacy of British law and repressive governments persist. These governments use their legal leverage "to impose regimes of self-censorship," said Lin Neumann of the Southeast Asia Press Alliance (SEAPA); the result is as effective, if less obvious, than direct state censorship. Economic obstacles also militate against independent (non-state) media development.

In Africa, for instance, endemic poverty has among its consequences poor educational opportunity, inadequate technological infrastructure, ethnic violence, and war. In Central and Eastern Europe, many of the powerful state broadcasters have yet to develop any meaningful public service governance or programming; independent news media in the region have been unable to make capital investments or pay adequate salaries, are often burdened by fines or taxes, and cannot afford to invest in staff training or development.

Other common problems that confront good journalism in emerging democracies include "envelope journalism," or bribery, and self-censorship in the name of national or cultural values. Governments sometimes use their power to purchase or withhold subsidies, usually in the form of advertising, in order to influence reporting.

Legal, cultural, or institutional buffers between journalism and government suppression are thin and few, and one of the most important institutional buffers, the judiciary, is often an instrument of the ruling party. Finally, threats to journalists' safety make independent reporting a very risky enterprise in many places. Reporters sans Frontieres, an NGO, reported that in 1998-99 nineteen journalists were killed worldwide. For the same period, the International Press Institute put the number killed at fifty.

Against realities such as these, the Aspen Institute conferees asked, what are the minimal enabling conditions necessary for a developing society to cultivate a free press or, more generally, public understanding and appreciation for free expression? And reciprocally, what tensions exist between the desire to promote freedom of expression and the desire to build a civil society? By what mechanisms, and by whom, are expressive freedoms-and especially press freedoms-to be balanced against social stability? Can there even be such a balancing, or are some social and political risks simply unavoidable in a free and open society?

In many developed nations these questions have been asked and, in one fashion or another, answered over a period of decades, sometimes centuries. The answers typically come by way of legal provisions-in constitutions, statutes, common law, and administrative law-and through the habits of journalism practice and cultural predilection. The confluence of these factors-law, journalistic practice, and cultural predilection-determines the balance of "freedom" and "responsibility" in a media system, and so while there may be some general principles of media development, there are few templates for their execution.

THEORY AND REALITY

The Aspen conferees began their deliberations with a discussion of free expression theory and the work of American legal scholar Thomas Emerson, whose justifications for limiting restrictions on speech fall into two broad and overlapping categories, the personal (or private) and the communal (or public). According to Emerson, free expression is important for the following reasons:

- Free expression allows people to develop their intellectual and spiritual faculties through their own activities and through engagement with others in art, religion, public affairs, and so on. The importance of free expression in this regard is made obvious by the experience of totalitarian regimes, where even in their private lives people must be wary of what they say and to whom, and even those who wish to conform-to say nothing of those who do not-have no choice in the matter.
- Free expression promotes the search for spiritual, intellectual, and civic truths, and these truths can best be discerned in an environment that allows all ideas to present themselves for debate. Here again the experience of totalitarian societies is instructive. Such societies often suppress not only political and cultural ideas, but scientific ones that conflict with official doctrine or the views of powerful institutions

like the army, the religious authorities, or a ruling political party. Clearly, in a society where some topics are off limits and others hold favoured positions, truth must take a tortured path to the light.

- Free expression is necessary for democratic self-governance. Obviously if the people are to be sovereign and free elections are to have any meaning, the people need to be able to assemble, to exchange ideas, and to circulate information related to public affairs. The press, in particular, must be free to investigate and criticize the government and to check abuses of state power, since even where governments are accepting of free expression they cannot be expected to use their powers to favour any interests but their own.
- Free expression works as a kind of social safety valve, and thus works better than suppression in maintaining social order. This view of free expression values tolerance both for its own sake and for its ability to channel dissent into peaceful social change. For the most part, conference participants accepted these justifications, but they also saw adherence to them as a luxury that few developing nations could afford. In some cases, they saw these justifications as cruel abstractions. As participant Ibrahim Nawar, chairman of Arab Press Freedom Watch, put it, "The right of survival comes before the right to free speech. In Iraq, for example, people are suffering and they would laugh at you if you talked about freedom of expression." Kabral Blay-Amihere, president of the West African Journalists Association, observed that on a daily basis in Ghana "consumers must choose between buying bread and buying a newspaper. Many people in my country make the equivalent of fifteen U.S. dollars per month."

More generally, when measured against the facts, Emerson's theoretical justifications have serious shortcomings even in stable democracies. It is not at all clear, for example, that "truth" results from an open and earnest search for the truth, and results matter. Americans may tolerate hate speech they find repulsive; Rwandans, Bosnians, and Kosovars have found it fatal. Must a free and open society accept the likelihood that some speech will be avowedly anti-democratic, and that some people will invariably find self-realization through expression that is antisocial?

Most of the participants thought not. Alexej Simonov, president of Russia's Glasnost Defense Foundation, described a false television news report aired in his country that resulted in an ethnic riot and several deaths and stated flatly that unrestrained expression is "absolutely unacceptable" when "freedom of expression becomes dangerous to the freedom of the country."

David Makali, director of Kenya's Media Institute and editor of Expression Today, expressed a similar view: "I have no doubt that freedom of expression requires some sort of regulation, since absolute freedom of expression has contributed to the destruction of societies such as Rwanda. The preservation of society depends on the promotion of progressive ideas over negative ones, and freedom of the press doesn't mean general public freedom of expression. Indeed, freedom of the press can work against the public's freedoms."

One danger in this view-which all the conferees recognized-is that a view of free expression that focuses narrowly on promoting stable self-government may be less tolerant of dissenting ideas in "nonpolitical" areas like art, literature, and religion-for many people the very things that make democracy worth supporting in the first place.

More generally, of course, the process of sorting out protected speech from unprotected speech is inevitably arbitrary and susceptible to- abuse.

Finally, as several conferees said, equating the mere fact of participation in the marketplace of ideas with meaningful decision-making on the part of all society's participants almost certainly claims too much. People everywhere link free speech with economic power, in developing societies and in the global media marketplace. Moreover, as media scholar James Carey has observed, societies with few legal restrictions may nonetheless have a system of expression controlled by a few powerful interests; restrictive, even authoritarian societies, may have a rich, flourishing-a more democratic, if less open-culture of expression and communication.

Perhaps the most useful insight from this part of the conferees' discussion was that there is no single underlying and unifying theory that supports freedom of expression, and more importantly, that no such theory is desirable. Indeed, it may be preferable from a social-acceptance point of view that free expression has not one justification but many, mutually reinforcing ones.

PRESS FREEDOM AND CIVIL SOCIETY

For many of the conferees the discussion about expression theory reduced to a practical question: Which is more urgent, establishing freedom of expression or establishing the conditions of civil society that make expression meaningful? Effectively circumventing the chicken and egg nature of the question, Sheila Coronel, executive director of the Philippine Centre for Investigative Journalism, put the matter this way:

It is a general thinking that freedom of expression is good for its own sake, regardless of the consequences. But, it doesn't guarantee anything. It doesn't guarantee fulfillment; it doesn't guarantee stability. We take the risk and we can have the exact opposite results of what we hope for. The social good that comes from free expression depends on social contexts-basic survival is necessary first or else free expression becomes a right of the elite. Many of us come from countries that lack a number of important enabling conditions-a diversity of media outlets, peace, and stability, a culture of tolerance, an economic system that meets people's basic needs. This raises some questions about what our role is as journalists.

How uu we use our freedoms to make free expression available to a majority of citizens?

Coronel's formulation of the issues fits well within the tradition of civil society thought, which is concerned with the institutions that comprise the non-governmental sector of society-churches, neighbourhoods, families, clubs, and civic groups, and so on. These institutions are characterized by voluntary association and perform a number of important social functions: they provide a buffer between the individual and the power of the state and the market; they create social capital; and they develop democratic values and habits.

Civil society, in short, provides to democracy what the law, with its rules and sanctions, cannot-social trust, social authority, civic virtue, and vision-the stuff of citizenship. It is an oversimplification, but not too much of one, to say that fundamentally civil society is about social responsibility.

This idea as it has developed in modern times stands in opposition to the Western tradition of liberal individualism and its tendency to see people either as bundles of legal rights and entitlements, cut off from any higher moral claims, or as consumers motivated only by economic self-interest.

Journalism, depending on how one defines the term, fits awkwardly into the mix of institutions that comprise civil society. One view of journalism sees its role as building civic consciousness and social solidarity (for example, the "public journalism" movement in the United States). A more traditional view-the so-called "fourth estate" view-follows closely on free expression theory and sees journalism as institutionalizing the expressive freedoms that provide a moderating influence on sources of power.

A third model of journalism, one often promoted with respect to developing nations, is less democratic than it is developmental; it sees journalism as promoting socio-economic change through education, economic expansion, and growth. This model is not necessarily anti-democratic, but places politics second to development, which is its priority.

In each of these models, journalism is a business, sometimes of a kind that links it financially or editorially to government. By being linked to government, journalism usually lacks the characteristic of voluntary association that defines civil society institutions. Ideally, however, journalism shares with those institutions devotion to a larger public purpose. Still, in a society where free association is possible, journalists have organized themselves into numerous voluntary associations whose broad purposes are to improve press performance and enhance public service.

Typically most of these organizations acknowledge that the corollary of press freedom is press responsibility, and some-press councils, for instance-also provide mechanisms for the public to hold journalists accountable for shoddy work.

With respect to responsibility, journalism again fits uneasily in traditional norms of civil society. To many journalists, and non-governmental organizations (NGOs) concerned with media, "responsibility" is a code word that signals government restrictions on media activity whenever the government deems such activity "irresponsible."

Several NGOs, for instance, have objected to the provision on free expression in the European Convention on Human Rights, which begins "Everyone has the right to freedom of expression," and continues "the exercise of these freedoms, since it carries with it duties and responsibilities, may be subject to such formalities, conditions, restrictions, or penalties as are prescribed by law and are necessary in a democratic society, in the interests of national security, territorial integrity or public safety, for the prevention of disorder or crime, for the protection of health or morals, for the protection of the reputation of the rights of others, for preventing the disclosure of information received in confidence, or for maintaining the authority and impartiality of the judiciary."

Despite the obvious potential for government abuse in such language, forty member countries of the Organization for Security and Cooperation in Europe (OSCE) subscribe to it. Many new democracies in Europe have used the same or similar language in drafting their media laws, and throughout the Aspen Institute conference several participants spoke-as Kwame Karikari, executive director of the Media Foundation for West Africa, did-of the need "to balance the rights of individual and community."

Most developed democratic governments officially view "freedom" as the result of non-restrictive government policies towards the media and "responsibility" as the product of self-regulation-a view that most of the journalists at the conference shared. However, in both established and emerging democracies, this principle probably works better in theory than it does in practice. One of the common features of an emerging democracy is an increasing number of people who call themselves journalists, but who are untrained and unprofessional. In both established and emerging democracies, the Internet exacerbates this trend.

Finally, in many developed media systems the ever widening acceptance of the marketplace as the best arbiter of press performance has led to greater reliance on sensational over serious journalism and many well publicized compromises in journalism ethics; not surprisingly, it has also led to renewed focus on press accountability. Presumably governments and journalists will in time mature and come to grips with their new freedoms, meanwhile, both must deal with the very real grievances and dangers that define the present.

Many journalists categorically reject the view that journalistic performance is in any way compromised by complete freedom in favour of a more absolutist approach to free expression. Americans in particular take this view, and indeed raised it in the 1997 negotiations with the Council of Europe that gave rise to the OSCE's creation of an office to promote freedom of the media. The United States' experience with free expression is unique in that to a degree unmatched anywhere the First Amendment protects speech that, in Supreme Court Justice Oliver Wendell Holmes' words, "we loathe and believe to be fraught with death."

Beyond the example of the First Amendment, the absolutist approach to free expression suffers from defects both as theory and as history. Despite Holmes' words (indeed, perhaps because of them) the American system of free expression is not absolutist, nor could it be.

All speech is conduct but not all conduct is speech, and taken literally, absolutism is unable to distinguish between the two. Thus absolutism not only makes a civil society impossible, but it plays into the hands of authoritarian governments that promise freedom of speech but arbitrarily punish dissenting or controversial speech as prohibited conduct.

Historically, the liberal American position on speech is relatively new. In the nineteenth century-the United States' own emerging democracy period-free speech law was state law, and state constitutions typically linked the right to speak freely with the obligation to speak responsibly. Beginning in 1931 and particularly since 1964, the United States Supreme Court has moved far from that view with respect to the press, but its legacy is still evident in some core doctrinal areas (prior restraint, for instance), and in the Court's respect for the police powers of the state (for example, the use of time, place, and manner restrictions).

Another feature of the American media system-and increasingly media systems everywhere-that runs counter to civil society thinking is its heavy reliance on the purchasing and viewing habits of consumers as the most credible measure of press performance. American journalism has historically eschewed critical evaluation both from within its ranks (ombudsmen and media critics) and from outside (commissions and academic studies); self-regulation is informal and, to the public, pretty much invisible.

This leaves the law as the only meaningful tool of redress for alleged press wrongs. The result, several legal commentators have noted, is ironic: It is primarily judges-officers of the state-who establish the de facto rules of press accountability in the United States, not the news media themselves. This enlarges the role of government in public life and strains it beyond its competency, both roles being anathema to civil society adherents. Whether for those reasons or others, participants at the conference saw self-regulation as a means of maintaining press independence from the state.

The conferees' opening discussions on free expression and civil society implicitly and repeatedly raised a straightforward question: What is it about journalism practice that makes it important to democracy, or in emerging societies, to democratization?

In the last decade, with the rise of what Lin Neumann called the "global democratization movement," a lot of money has been spent on media development on the assumption that it is essential to democracy, but without much thought about the forms that either journalism or democracy might take. There have been a number of scholarly studies on media systems in the post-Cold War period, most of them descriptive. Professor Guy Berger of Rhodes University in South Africa conceptually categorized media systems into four variants:

- Liberal, or the classic Fourth Estate model, in which journalism is an independent source of social power that provides a check on both state and private power. The liberal model sees journalism primarily as a private enterprise rather than a state one, and as such, the common criticism is that its independence is too easily compromised by private interests-owners, advertisers, public relations firms, and others.
- Neoliberal, in which journalism is the primary advocate for cultural pluralism, giving voice to minority and dissident voices against the dominant political views in the media system. The neoliberal model is premised on public debate, and in much of the world has been a response to authoritarian political regimes.
- Social democratic, in which journalism performs a public role more akin to guide than guardian. In this view, journalists do not stand in an adversarial role to power so much as frame the terms of citizenship,

define and shape democratic culture. Large public-service state broadcasters like the BBC or NHK epitomize the social democratic model.

- Participatory, in which journalism is neither guide nor guardian, but actively promotes the voluntary associations and political habits of civil society. Where social democratic journalism concerns itself with the formation of the nation, participatory journalism concerns itself with the formation of communities.

And unlike neoliberal journalism, which sees citizens primarily as consumers of politics, the participatory model sees them as political actors. Participatory journalism is relatively new; it is exemplified in the United States by the public journalism movement, and around the world by attempts to use the Internet has a tool of political organization and action.

These models overlap in some obvious ways. Many state broadcasters, for example, see themselves not merely as nurturing their nation's culture, but also as serving as a watchdog on government (liberal model) and, as many state broadcasters are required to do, giving voice to minority viewpoints (neoliberal model). Similarly, those who see journalism as a Fourth Estate are likely to believe that their work increases public knowledge and thus makes citizen participation in government meaningful.

These models are useful as tools of analysis because they function differently in developing democracies than they do in developed ones. In developed nations, for instance, it is increasingly difficult to see how some of these models function except as idealized norms.

Throughout the developed world, journalism has become a small part of a larger media environment that includes entertainment, sports, music, advertising, and direct marketing.

As other Aspen Institute papers have noted, the mixing of content and purpose puts journalism in an increasingly competitive environment, thus privileging news content that is easily leveraged across multiple media platforms. These trends are amplified by globalization and media deregulation, both of which have unleashed additional competitive forces. The liberal journalism tradition is not dead-it lives in some elite media and also in some decidedly un-elite media, primarily on the Internet, that report on both public affairs and on the failings of the Fourth Estate.

In much of the developing world, the liberal journalistic tradition is not only alive and kicking, but owes its existence to the very factors that repress it-especially inept or corrupt governments. Participants noted the irony that in many of the societies represented at the conference, journalism was in key respects better when it was officially suppressed. In some cases, said Sheila Coronel, good journalism that survived in the worst of political and social conditions now has to succeed financially against competition from a variety of other outlets, including many that trade in entertainment and sensationalism. "Tyranny of the state may be better than tyranny of the market," she said. "As journalists we knew what to do with the state-you topple it. But what do you do with the market?"

Liberal and Neoliberal Journalism in Developing Societies Coronel's question gets at an important problem: For journalists in developing societies, the liberal and neoliberal journalistic traditions are not necessarily conducive to democratization. The liberal tradition, for example, supports vigorous and effective monitoring of the government, and its emphasis on private ownership provides a needed counterweight to what are often government-held monopolies in media. The neoliberal push for pluralism is also essential to democratization, if not also to civil society.

However, there is nothing about the liberal model that makes it inherently democratic, and as several participants at the conference argued, the ethical excesses of the liberal model may undermine public support for free expression. Maciej Wierzynski, director of Voice of America's Polish Service, described a situation in which Poland's two small private television networks have curried political favour in order to insulate themselves from competition. "One of the private networks," he said, "bribed the whole parliamentary caucus to preserve the 30 percent limit on foreign investment and block the flow of foreign capital to the media market."

Private media can subvert democratic impulses in other ways as well. If, for instance, the media see their role primarily as promoting economic development or social stability, they can devolve into nothing more than a mouthpiece for an undemocratic government. The effect is to further entrench established interests, in government and in the private sector. Participant Rosa María Alfaro of the Asociación de Comunicadores Sociales (CALANDRIA) of Peru said that in Latin America "political parties and government buy journalists with advertising," effectively securing favorable treatment through patronage.

Basma El Husseiny, a Ford Foundation program officer based in Egypt, made a similar observation about journalists in her country, and characterized some as "mercenaries."

At the other extreme, liberal journalism can threaten democratization when it becomes a source of political opposition in its own right or, as often happens, when a nominally independent press becomes the tool of politicians opposed to the government, as happened with the late Massoud Abiola in Nigeria. When this happens, journalistic values are subverted to political agendas, even more so when the opposition press scores a victory at the ballot box and then becomes the government press-and thus loses its liberal character entirely, to the point where it may retard or subvert democratization.

In developing media systems, globalization and deregulation have also been a mixed bag. Deregulation has often meant an exchange of one monopoly (government) with another (private), as in Russia, where virtually all the nation's non-government media are now controlled by about three large industrial conglomerates; this oligopoly is closely linked to sources of political and economic power and thus has found it hard to resist government threats and pressure. While globalization has led to some foreign investment in developing nations, such investment does not always translate into greater diversity of content and often has the effect of diminishing domestic programming in favour of imported American programming.

Globalization in developing societies has also meant the involvement of NGOs and outside funders, which have their own social and political agendas. From the point of view of those on the receiving end of such aid, it was clear from discussion at the conference that much of it-no matter what its source or the motivations behind it-was misdirected and some utterly wasteful.

Indonesian journalist Andreas Harsono argued, to general agreement, that many international organizations are considerably more concerned with their own interests than in the needs of those whom they purport to serve.

At worst, he said, some NGOs exist only to perpetuate themselves, and others, even when they mean well, "are not always helpful and sometimes are presumptuous. The people they send do not know a country's culture or history. Many international NGOs do not have a long-standing interest or purpose in a country and so do nothing to build local capacity. They often bypass local democratic processes, and so do not solve problems but make them worse."

Illustrating Harsono's point, Kabral Blay-Amihere, president of the West African Journalists Association, described a £15,000 British training program in Ghana in which, he charged, only £2,000 went to actual training-the rest went to overhead, including the cost of supporting two tutors sent from the United Kingdom. Lin Neumann told of an NGO operating in Southeast Asia that received a $500,000 grant for no other reason than that the grantor was under deadline pressure to find a grantee.

While the conferees did not discuss it at length, they seemed to agree that one reason for the clumsiness of Western aid is that it is often driven by the so-called "CNN effect"-the process by which international attention, governmental and non-governmental, is focused on a region by virtue of television news coverage. "The response to crisis is then often blown out of proportion," said Sharmini Peries, executive director of the Canadian Journalists Association, which operates the International Freedom of Expression Exchange. "There is a flood of support and afterward there is total abandonment."

The consequences of the intervention may nonetheless linger, said Basma El Husseiny: "International agencies reorder the priorities, sometimes harmfully." The aid and development community's perspective on these issues received little attention at the conference, since no one was there to represent it, but a few points seem obvious. NGOs and IGOs can indeed become large, agenda-driven institutions that need to maintain a funding base; they can be competitive and even counterproductive. That does not mean the people working for them are always inexperienced or unknowledgeable quite the contrary.

Moreover, those working in the field can spend an inordinate amount of time negotiating with political, cultural, and military authorities at the local, national, and occasionally, international level, making even incremental changes difficult. In this regard, errors of fact and outright misrepresentations by journalists are problems for the aid community, particularly in regions where media are themselves divided into warring camps.

Finally, the value of any particular program-despite the division between "real training" and "overhead"-will always be subjective. If anything, this part of the conference discussion underscored the importance of donor priorities to the flow of international aid, but offered little of value to say about it.

JOURNALISM IN DEVELOPING SOCIETIES

In developed media systems, one response to globalization and to the excesses of the liberal journalism model has been to give renewed emphasis to the social democratic model typified by public broadcasting.

Speaking at the spring conference, the Aspen Institute's Charles Firestone asked whether governments could not play a valuable role in facilitating and safeguarding diversity of expression, and particularly in the modern era, whether government might not be a necessary countervailing force against the large concentrations of private economic power in the media marketplace.

Through direct or indirect intervention, government may-among other things-promote public access to the means of communication, encourage and regulate competition, and subsidize high-quality news, public affairs, and cultural fare that the market may not support.

Participants had mixed feelings about the government's ability to play a positive role in news and public affairs. Even where governments are ostensibly acting in the "public interest," said Maciej Wierzynski, the legacy of state control makes for an uneasy partnership.

"Anytime we try to discuss the role of government in media it leads to political questions," he said. "Who controls? Who sets the priorities? In the case of Poland, state-owned media have played the decisive role in electronic media on the rationale that they are protecting 'national culture' against foreign television. As a result, we have a situation where national culture is not so much protected, but the government makes political appointments to state radio and television."

It is not uncommon for journalists in democratizing nations to reject the social democratic journalism model, which in their experience has been used primarily as a tool of domination. But more recent experience with privatization has led some to modify this view: Albeit imperfect, government involvement in the news media at least allows for public scrutiny and accountability. Discussing the possibility of privatization of state broadcasting in Ghana, Kwame Karikari worried that privatization would result in a system peopled by "cronies" of the ruling party.

"If broadcasting is still a civil service, we can demand that it really serve the public interest. If it is just a front, we can do nothing."

PARTICIPATORY JOURNALISM

Participatory journalism-much scorned in developing nations-has obvious appeal in developing societies. It emphasizes the kinds of civic associations that promote civil society, and in societies emerging from authoritarian pasts no single institution can advance the cause of democratization. Participatory journalism also reaches out to the large numbers of people, particularly in rural areas, who have traditionally been both socially marginalized and beyond the reach of virtually every public affairs medium except state radio.

Critics of participatory journalism charge that it is susceptible to abuse. This may be especially true in societies without a tradition of independent media. Further, the impediments to independent journalism in developing societies-poverty, high illiteracy rates, scattered populations, and poor infrastructure-are particularly injurious to the goals of participatory journalism.

The Internet, for example, has been widely praised as the first mass medium that allows for interactivity and community building-and thus ideally suited to participatory journalism-but poverty and limited information infrastructure make the Internet unavailable to a majority of people in many developing societies.

The Role for International Organizations in Promoting Free Press and Civil Society

Because so many of the conference participants were from the international development community, a great deal of discussion focused on what international organizations could do to support the enabling conditions of press freedom and civil society. Generally, the participants agreed that IGOs and NGOs need to place greater emphasis on local and regional programs that will sustain themselves after crises and start-up funding are passed.

Indigenous media, in turn, must better identify and articulate their own needs to the international community. Specifically, the conferees identified two categories of need that require focused attention: infrastructure development and professional development (training and institutional support) for journalists. The two are in some obvious ways mutually supporting and, as discussed below, the participants thought of professional development as less an exercise in instruction than one in social engineering, in building the civil society.

Infrastructure Support

Some infrastructure needs are clearly material ones. Particularly in societies in conflict, said Kwame Karikari, "Media houses have become targets, as in Sierra Leone and Liberia." International organizations, he urged, should make capital investments if they want to make a lasting difference. "Invest in a printing press and get a journalistic organization to run it as an independent company," he said. "Support it with management training." Such investments do not have to be large.

Still another material need identified by several participants-and one clearly linked to journalism professionalism-are journalism schools. In some developing regions, Central Europe and Russia especially, journalism schools tend to be highly theoretical places staffed by professors with little newsroom experience and almost no practical knowledge of free-enterprise journalism. Upgrading these institutions, or inventing new ones, is a key to building a level of professionalism that well-meaning but short-lived programs cannot.

As Sheila Coronel of the Philippines Centre for Investigative Journalism said, "We need support that's not a seminar here or there, but where you identify intellectuals in a region and you equip them with books and other materials, and some pay, and you let them teach."

David Makali appeared to second this view: "I hold a dim view of short-term training programs. After you train people they disappear and results disappear. It would be better to invest in self-teaching aids, in education as part of infrastructure. I would like to see resource centers that journalists can access and that are stocked with materials for self-teaching."

Several participants did mention training programs they thought valuable, such as a World Bank project on health issues in developing nations that was coupled with an extensive reporting project. Lin Neumann described successful efforts in Thailand to first pass a national open-records law, then to train journalists how to use it.

Andreas Harsono argued for specialized reporting programs that would provide journalists substantive expertise in several areas-health care, the military, religion, and finance. Another need that might be considered under infrastructure is simple protection. Journalists who are subject to harassment, physical harm, or expulsion need both somewhere to go and a way to publicize their plight.

A number of participants urged the creation of organizations or facilities that would provide physical relief and professional support to journalists in such situations.

ETHICS AND SELF-REGULATION

Three participants-Andreas Harsono, Charles Onyango-Obbo, and Rosa María Alfaro-offered short expositions on the problems affecting journalistic practice in Indonesia, Uganda, and Peru, respectively. In each case the problems were different but the result the same-a lack of professionalism and widespread public distrust of the news media.

Harsono described an explosion of news and information outlets in Indonesia since the collapse of the Suharto regime, but rued the fact that thousands of people are now working as journalists who have no training and worse, no sense of reporting standards or ethics. Many are simply advocates for a particular political or religious point of view, and a huge number-approximately 80 percent, Harsono said, routinely take bribes for stories, a practice euphemistically known as "envelope journalism."

Obbo, editor of Uganda's largest independent newspaper, The Monitor, described a situation in Uganda (which also occur in other parts of Africa) where leading news outlets are owned by the ruling elite and where journalists sometimes seek to become celebrities through arrest or detention rather than through the quality of their reporting. In Peru, Alfaro said, the state intelligence apparatus keeps a watchful eye on journalists and is not shy about using physical intimidation or torture to silence critics. Many reporters and news organizations thus find life easier and more profitable if they curry favour with the political establishment. Not surprisingly, 60 percent of Peru's people do not believe what they read or hear in the news.

At one level, of course, the need is for basic training in journalism ethics. As Alexej Simonov put it, "In countries in transition, journalists themselves don't always know good from bad practice." The caution for international organizations investing in media development is that Simonov's distinction may not be so easy to draw. In much of Central Europe and Russia, for instance, commentary, not even-handed reporting, is the prevailing form of news. In the aftermath of communism, the first impulse of those with newfound freedoms has been to express points of view long suppressed, not always to report public events dispassionately.

Commentary as news is also a legacy of the communist period, during which journalists wishing to show their independence from the ruling party would frequently pepper their reports with sardonic remarks. It is not so clear that this legacy suits democratization or the development of a new, liberal media system.

The short experience of NTV, until recently the lone private television network in Russia, makes the point. NTV had at various times been fiercely covetous of its independence from government censorship, as in its coverage of the 1994 war in Chechnya, and at other times shamelessly allied with the government, as in its support of Boris Yeltsin's 1996 presidential campaign. Understandable as NTV's actions may have been from a political perspective, they nonetheless undermined its claim to the liberal tradition of journalistic practice and opened the network to charges that its editorial choices are politically motivated.

In debt to economically powerful interests, NTV found itself harassed both by creditors and by government officials in 2000. Vladimir Gusinsky, whose MOST consortium controlled NTV until recently, was forced in late summer of 2000 to sell his stake in the company to Gazprom, a state-owned utility company. Moreover, at the time of publication of this report, Gusinsky is under House arrest in Spain and fighting extradition to Russia where he faces criminal fraud charges, thus raising the question of whether vigorous, independent media can survive under the Putin government.

Conference discussion of journalism ethics moved naturally to the question of press self-regulation and public accountability, subjects that the participants saw in practical terms. Most of the participants thought that developing accountability in the practice of journalism is key to building civil society-a case of leading by example. A second justification for self-regulation was that it provides a bulwark against arbitrary or repressive state intervention.

Self-regulation, of course, takes many forms. Internally it can include ombudsmen; Op-Ed and letters pages in newspapers; "rights of reply," including statutory ones; and various forms of research or community outreach that allow news organizations to monitor public attitudes about all manner of things, including the performance of the press. All of these mechanisms were at least mentioned at the conference, though few were discussed at any length.

Andreas Harsono, for example, spoke favorably of a right-of-reply in which people claiming to be harmed by news reports would be able to respond in a place or manner (depending on the medium) as prominent as the one in which the damage was done. Rosa María Alfaro, who had talked earlier about using quantitative studies of public attitudes toward journalists, spoke favorably about an experiment in civic journalism in which she had participated.

A more vigorous discussion followed on the subject of external forms of self-regulation-for example professional journalism associations and press councils. Several participants who favoured these mechanisms argued as David Makali did, that professional associations can "assure ethics and monitor practice, and so help to avoid government interventions." Some participants noted that journalism associations of one kind or another (unions, for instance) were already in existence in their countries but that they did little to make journalism better and in some cases were an obstacle to improvement.

Convincing journalists that their existing standards are low and their monitoring mechanisms toothless (or worse) may be a hard sell, said Kwame Karikari, but it has to be done: "Nobody will achieve anything if journalists themselves are not convinced of the need. We need reform both at the level of professional associations and at the level of each media organization, where there needs to be in-house codes and ethics training."

Interestingly, the sticking point in this discussion turned on the question of who qualifies as a journalist and how external-monitoring associations should be organized. Lin Neumann of the Southeast Asia Press Alliance (SEAPA) summarized the problem: "Strong national associations of journalists linked into regional networks are important and provide the framework to support [self-regulation]. But the key word here is 'independent.' Many regional journalism bodies have been dominated by journalists from countries that don't have a free press. You must recognize that membership for what it is and keep independent media separate from state-owned media. SEAPA was created to focus attention on countries in Southeast Asia that have a free press, because our experience was that there was no regional voice that united independent press advocacy organizations into one network."

A number of journalists at the conference observed, as Joseph Gitari, program officer for Eastern and Southern Africa for the Ford Foundation did, that the problem of organizing journalists in societies where many work for state-owned media is "very divisive."

Some journalists expressed doubt that they could even make the distinction between independent journalists and others. For example, said David Makali, "It is not at all uncommon for journalists to identify with the ownership of the media houses" for which they work. Are such people independent? Further, many civil society organizations (women's groups, AIDS prevention groups, etc.) are themselves in the media business, publishing materials on a variety of important topics. Are these people journalists?

All agreed that defining independence merely in terms of one's employment is insufficient; more important is independence in service to the public interest, though the principle offers little guidance on how to organize journalists professionally. Perhaps, as Kabral Blay-Amihere said, "It is better to carry everybody along, to use one umbrella to advance issues of press freedom."

Price and Neumann also asked whether the whole attempt to organize journalists, along any sort of criteria, did not raise the possibility of state "licensing" of journalists. Surprisingly, this issue received little discussion from the conferees, in part, it seemed, because of the view many expressed that self-regulation would preclude government regulation.

Models exist that would support such a view, particularly in Europe, where twenty-five nations have both a press council and a professional code of journalism ethics, and nine other nations have at least a code of ethics. (Regarding broadcasting, many press councils are official state bodies, but they are excluded from this count.)

Press councils have two main jobs: to protect the rights of the public by giving it an opportunity to complain about bad journalism and to investigate these complaints; and to protect the news media themselves from government regulation and from meddling by powerful private interests. Most press councils have both journalists and media owners as members; a few include academics as members.

At the other extreme on this subject is the American view. American journalists typically resist any but the most vague codes of conduct for fear that someone-whether the government, a public official, or an angry subject of a news story-will attempt to use the code against them in a lawsuit.

Indeed, there have been a couple of notable instances (including one that landed in the United States Supreme Court) in which judges have turned what journalists thought were voluntary ethics guidelines into mandatory court orders.

For this reason and others, United States news organizations, led prominently by the New York Times, killed through neglect a short-lived National Press Council.

Despite all this, American journalists (and Western journalists in general) are organized into every imaginable kind of association-by medium, by position in the newsroom or in management, by reportorial specialty, by region and state, and so on. Many of these organizations do concern themselves with best practices, and some explicitly with ethics.

Some are organized specifically to militate against government intervention, and many will provide financial and legal support to redress actions they perceive to be limitations on or violations of press freedom.

Many notable observers of international media agree with the views expressed at the Aspen Institute conference that journalism associations, because they foster collaboration, are useful in presenting a united front against government restrictions.

Finally, a key point raised by several of the conferees is that journalism associations must be, wherever possible, inclusive of ethnic and racial minorities. Given the nature of conflict present in many of the nations represented at the conference, the recommendation is an important one for civil society and the press.

Ibrahim Nawar agreed: "Newsrooms must be multicultural, with a good reflection of ethnicity, culture, and gender. This is an issue of credibility."

CONCLUSION

Under the rubric of civil society, the conferees at the Aspen Institute's first international roundtable on journalism brought their focus to bear on questions of freedom from state intervention, and the development of journalistic professionalism and communications infrastructure.

Given the composition of the conference group-journalists and foundation program officers-attention naturally fell on the role that journalists and international organizations could or should play in thinking creatively about the challenges in these areas.

Future Aspen Institute international roundtables on journalism will presumably wish to look more closely at strategic opportunities for media development. In anticipation of those meetings, a number of issues need more systematic and, where possible, quantitative examination.

The first issue that needs more examination concerns journalism and media aid, which predictably has mirrored the pattern of Western aid generally. That pattern can be described as "aid to end aid," in the words of the Marshall Plan, and at its worst has had a quick-fix mentality that avoids the kinds of careful need-specific planning and patience that are really required.

This is partly the result, as the conferees noted, of concentrating too much aid on just a few countries, a tendency that fuels frustrations on the side of the aid giver and receiver. Developing nations, owing to unreceptive governments, weak economies, and inadequate infrastructure, cannot, as one commentator has written, be stuffed with development "the way you stuff corn into a goose."

Finally, some regions, such as Africa, get very little media aid compared to nations in Central Europe. Drawing attention to this imbalance and working to rectify it is a task for journalists and for international organizations. A second issue that needs further examination concerns the role that journalists could or should play in educating the international aid community about journalism.

As the Ford Foundation's John Phillip Santos and Larry Cox pointed out during the conference, the international aid community is relatively new to and inexperienced with media aid. So, journalists need to develop a much more sophisticated understanding of IGOs and NGOs, what they do and, more importantly perhaps, what their limitations are.

NGOs, for instance, now deliver more assistance each year than the United Nations does (not counting the assistance of the World Bank and the International Monetary Fund). But aid overall has declined around the world in the 1990s, and some of the infrastructure problems identified at the Aspen Institute conference-poverty, for instance-cannot be fixed by the trickle of aid that goes to them.

It seems unlikely that international organizations can provide, on a sustained basis, such essential public functions as education, health care, or housing. In so far as these things create the enabling conditions for civil society and press freedom, civil society and press freedom may remain precarious things in many parts of the world. Even where living conditions improve, civil society is not the same as, nor is it a substitute for, democratically accountable governance. IGOs and NGOs cannot provide such governance and, as their critics often point out, they are themselves unaccountable.

One key lesson from the conference, then, is that for media assistance to be effective journalists themselves need to take a leadership role in conceiving it and carrying it out. Further, journalists should urge international organizations to coordinate their efforts more effectively. One possible approach is to utilize the World Wide Web site IJN.org, operated by the International Centre for Journalists; the site posts information on the lessons learned from media development programs, reports who is doing what, and lists knowledgeable contacts in the field.

Intergovernmental organizations (IGOs) may be more likely to cooperate than nongovernmental organizations

(NGOs) will, but based on the comments made at the conference, NGOs could and should do better. Funders could give a- boost to such coordination and collaboration by insisting on it as a requirement for funding.

Above all, journalists need to think more strategically about the ends that aid should serve-about what kind of journalism is desirable for what kind of society. One way to do that, at conference tables and elsewhere, is to broaden the base of knowledge about international journalism, to include scholars, policy makers, and others whose experience and ideas can more fully inform the effort to build a civil society and advance the process of democratization.

8

MEDIA CONVERGENCE, DIVERSITY, DEMOCRACY AND POLITICS

INTRODUCTION

The complexity of democracy is both its defect and its virtue. As an idealized conception, democracy promotes equitable social order through the counterplay of interests while the rule of law protects individual citizens from the arbitrariness of the state. In practice, matters are considerably more ambiguous.

Contradictions exist between theory and action; the power and privileges of some people invariably make them "more equal" than others—social equity being a relative term. Even so, belief that democracy renders "the greatest good for the greatest number" constitutes the orthodox faith of contemporary civil religion. "No one pretends that democracy is perfect or all wise," noted Winston Churchill in his oft-quoted observation. "Indeed, it has been said that democracy is the worst form of government, except for all the others that have been tried from time to time."

What happens to this delicately poised mechanism, however, if public channels of communication cease to provide the free flow of substantive information deemed critical to keeping democracy's inner workings lubricated?

The elegance of the system resides in the ultimate authority of a rational citizenry to restrain unwise action. For this "failsafe" check to work—whether the political model is of a plebiscite of individuals or coalitions of pluralistic interest groups—the voters need to know the facts. As we enter the first years of the twenty-first century, however, this underlying fundamental upon which the system is poised—access to information—has become too uncertain to take for granted.

In the intervening centuries since Locke, Montisquieu, and Jefferson posited the intellectual foundations for modern democracy, history has shown how thin is the social membrane that separates civil rule from tyranny. Securing the vitality of democratic processes is an ongoing challenge; each generation faces unexpected developments that put at risk the orderly processes of the preceding era. In our day, unprecedented advances in communication technology are rewiring (literally and metaphorically) the social landscape. Formats, transmission modes, and even media that we no longer consider novel were largely unheard-of as recently as a decade ago.

In the wake of instantaneous, ubiquitous transmission of voice and data, new issues arise. Some are economic, some legal, and some moral. The way the political system—itself being affected by the new technology—responds will have profound implications on how democracy evolves.

Although we are in only the earliest stages of this communications transformation, prophets foresee it unleashing revolutionary change. "The Internet isn't just another media delivery system, like television and radio before it," writes Katherine Fulton in the Columbia Journalism Review. "It's the catalyst for a historic transition from one era to another. In the same way that the steam engine produced the train, which accelerated the shift to an industrial age, so will the Internet—or what we now call the Internet—slowly absorb every other communications medium over the next few decades, and abolish-old notions of time and space." At the same time, as technology converges the structure of the communication industry is in the throes of consolidation. Both dynamics affect how the media function. The issue is whether these changes bode ill or well for democracy.

The question is open-ended. Business imperatives will play an important role in determining the outcome. The hypothetical powers of the new media risk head-on collision with the harsh calculus of financial viability. The dot-com implosion provides an example of how new technology-driven communication sectors explode on the scene with the brilliance of a supernova only to collapse into themselves like a black hole. While the life cycle of the technology itself remains ascendant, specific applications along the arc may prove less lasting than originally predicted, particularly if they are forced to rely on commerce to survive.

As a consequence, political entities—communities, agencies, and nations—will play a considerable role in influencing how the new technologies fare. A host of issues lend themselves to possible state intervention: Should the market for services be wholly unfettered or regulated? Do paradigms of competition need to be revised? Should content be privatized or communal? Are the interests of the media aligned or discordant with the interests of the public? Needless to say, there are no simple answers.

To address these issues and related questions, the Aspen Institute Communications and Society Program convened a group of chief executive officers (CEOs) and other top-level executives from leading communications and technology companies, the investment community, government, foundations, academia, and the nonprofit sector for its annual

Forum on Communications and Society (FOCAS), August 4–7, 2002 in Aspen, Colorado. The three-day conference, "Media Convergence, Diversity, and Democracy: Survival in the New Media Environment," explored media convergence and its impact on the survival of media companies, the diversity of voices, and the health of democracies in the post–September 11th world.

Moderated by Charles M. Firestone, executive director of the Aspen Institute Communications and Society Program, the discussions centered around formulating policy recommendations to government, business, and other leaders that will leverage the tools and powers of the media, old and new. This report is a synthesis and interpretation of those discussions. The report is written from the perspective of an informed observer at the conference. Unless attributed to a particular person, the comments contained in this report should not be taken as embodying the views or carrying the endorsement of any specific participant at the conference.

DEMOCRACY AND THE COMMUNICATION IMPERATIVE

Democracy as we have come to understand it today is as much a cultural construct as a system of governance. As such, it eludes rigorous definition. On one hand it can be described in terms of formal aspects: distribution of authority, electoral rights, statutes, courts and the like. As important as these arrangements, however, is an archetypal idea in the popular mind of democracy as a promise of possibility. The promise means different things to different people.

To some it is freedom of individual autonomy, to others the notion of communal responsibility. ("You have the Republican and Democratic definitions of opportunity,"

Nicholas Lehman observed about the United States. "The Republican is 'right to choose' and the Democrat is 'everyone gets a chanee.'")

To focus exclusively on the institutional characteristics of democracy is to ignore its appeal to the emotions—particularly telling in an era characterized by fewer people going to the polls each year and more people expressing disaffection from their own government. In appraising the impact of the new communications technology on the prospects of democracy, both aspects—the "hard" and the "soft"—must be considered. The hard side of democracy addresses the way institutions function and whether they will become more efficient, more equitable, and more responsive.

This aspect has to do with concrete results and access to information. Is it probable, for example, that as an elected representative and his or her constituents become more interactively linked, they will be more attentive to each other's responses at each stage of the legislative process? Will the criteria of administrative and executive decision making become more transparent? Will broadband make accessible to concerned parties in a timelier manner the ongoing governmental proceedings that affect them? Will the courts be able to speed the flow of cases and rendering of justice through innovative communications?

The second category is subjective—difficult to measure but ultimately, perhaps, even more significant. This aspect has to do with the "promise" of democracy as interpreted by various factions and whether the new media enhance confidence among these factions that their vision of the good society is being realized meaningfully. In addition to being conduits of content, the new communications increasingly are being understood to constitute the embodiment of community itself.

Networks of linked users are replacing what social scientists used to call interpersonal primary groups. John Dewey, the classic American social philosopher, spoke to this version of democracy when he celebrated the fusion of separate interests into a communal will ("a society in which the ever-expanding and intricately ramifying consequences of associated activities shall be known in the full sense of that word, so that an organized, articulate Public comes into being.") Dewey wrote this description when radio was cutting-edge. In examining a landscape in which the town square has been replaced by the chat room, we must transpose the language Dewey used to ask whether the commonwealth ideal lends itself to embodiment in digital form.

Democracy's interactive nature, the interplay between the governed and their governors, is one of its salient characteristics. Media serve as the open circuit loop that facilitates this communication in various applications that further this end. Arguments for freedom of the media have been etched into the fabric of the Constitution to protect these channels. An important rationale for First Amendment sanctions is to give the media the latitude to translate the rush of events into comprehensible, informed points of view. The presumption is that competitive media will provide competitive perspectives and that democracy is best served in this marketplace of ideas. Will this premise remain true in the wake of media convergence and industry concentration?

WHAT IS DEMOCRACY?

Tracy Westen, vice chair and CEO of the Centre for Governmental Studies, offered a salient overview of democracy as a context within which to examine the political impact of the media. Sketching out a rudimentary typography, Westen noted two essential types of democracy:

"citizen democracy," in which individuals decide things directly (e.g., when individuals assemble in deliberative sessions akin to the New England town meeting or when they vote on a ballot measure) and; "representative democracy," in which individuals vote for representatives who then derive authority as members of groups that exercise power for them.

Since the Greeks originated democracy, a fundamental debate has waged about who is qualified to govern. The poles of the argument pit "the people" against what is offered as a more qualified elite.

"Over the last 3500 years," noted Westen, "there has been a division that dates back to when Plato contended that governing was too difficult for ordinary people—and thus the ideal ruler was a 'philosopher king'—and Aristotle countered with the proposition that ordinary citizens could be trained to participate in democracy. In the formative days of the United States, Alexander Hamilton argued that it was necessary to put power in the hands of truly capable individuals, leaders and business figures who have proven themselves in the market. Thomas Jefferson said, no, you have to trust the people and thus educate them so they are capable of exercising power themselves."

The dialogue continues into the present. "We have in a sense a 'two-part democracy,'" observed Westen, calling the current American system a hybrid. "One part is a representative democracy, in which we elect delegates to do the work for us—presidents, congressmen, senators, city council members, and so forth. We also have a growing system of direct democracy in which we vote directly on matters; half the states have initiative ballot measures."

In both modes public opinion constitutes a strong influence of direct democracy, whether it is expressed in the midst of elections or during the intervals between them.

"Some citizens feel that once you participate in an election, that's all you need to do," Westen continued. "You vote every two, four, or six years, then go about your business, and two, four, or six years later you decide how well your elected officials did, up or down. But most people feel that government policies are too important to be left only to elections and thus try to participate in various ways throughout the year."

This participation can take such forms as membership in activist groups, contributions, organized lobbying, or writing letters to the editor—all of which contribute to the expression of public opinion. It is in this area—preparing citizens for an election and preparing them to participate in ongoing politics—that Westen suggests the media plays its most prominent democratic role.

"Media" itself is something of a cumbersome term, suggesting a singular entity—which in fact is not the case. "Very simplistically, I find it useful to divide media into two types," noted Westen.

The first is journalistically mediated media: newscasts and entertainment pieces and so forth. In this respect, media is a tightly controlled form that tells the audience what is important, according to the viewpoint and priorities of each specific organization. The second type of media serves as a platform that allows one individual to speak directly to another individual. Telephone is this kind of medium, as are e-mail, websites, or over-the air talk shows.

"In a sense," Westen said, "the media is an intermediary between the specific and the general. The public will never have the time or inclination or perhaps even the ability to understand the details of issues at a deep level. But they do understand at a broader level: Will my taxes go up? Am I making a choice between pollution and national defense? Is this policy good or bad for my child's education?"

Why, then, do we have democracy?" asked Westen in summary, "and how do media serve those ends?" He suggested four reasons:

- We have democracy so people can participate in the affairs around them. The role of the media in this respect is to portray people who are doing just that—to show how the process is taking place.
- We have democracy because it constitutes a better fit than any other system between public opinion and actual implemented policies. Media in this case provides a link between citizens and representatives; it communicates public opinion to decision makers.
- Democratic societies arrive at truth more effectively than other systems. The marketplace of ideas is sloppy and messy, but it works so that democratic societies tend to come up with better policies than those that rest on arbitrary rules. The goal of media here is to offer education, ideas, and opinions.
- Finally, the role of media is to protect democracy against alternative forms, against tearing apart or deteriorating into authoritarianism. In this sense, the media acts as a watchdog; it provides warnings that your civil liberties are in jeopardy or there are scandals in the operations of the government.

Westen cited several conditions in the present environment that prevent the media from fully performing these functions. One issue, ironically, is the abundance of media. "We have vast sources of information, extraordinary access to facts, everything you might want in a democracy. The problem is that people are using these sources of media less and less." As an example, he cited the suspension by the Federal Communications Commission (FCC) in the 1980s of the rule that every broadcast radio station had to do at least five minutes of news an hour.

A second problem has to do with inadequate local coverage. "When we get down to city council and supervisor elections, the voters don't have a clue who these people are. There's been a systemic failure of media at the local level." Finally, alluding to media's "platform" role, Westen cited the problem of "year-round participation" in the political process. "We clearly have the desire of citizens to participate between elections in the day-to-day process, but we do not have media mechanisms that allow them to do that effectively."

As Westen observed, "Media is almost the guardian of the quality of the integrity in our democratic system. The role of the old media—print, television, and radio—has evolved over time so that it is generally understood what is expected of them. There is serious debate whether they adequately discharge their obligation, but there is not much disagreement amongst media leaders about what they are supposed to do. In the best traditions of their trade, the media serve 'the culture of public duty.'

The essence of this culture is a shared trust on the parts of both the public and the profession that journalism exercises a responsibility to inform and educate and occasionally even bear witness to things that matter." As would be expected owing to its youth, the new media have been considerably less tested than the old media with respect to the laws under which it operates—particularly those pertaining to the applicability of the First Amendment. Nor have the rights of the public to access the new media been addressed.

PUBLIC TRUST IN THE MEDIA

As the idea of democracy spreads and the proportion of the world's population that is exercising democratic forms grows, governance of media becomes increasingly important.

Various elements that sustain democracy—most notably respect for the rule of law—depend on a vigilant, informed public. New technologies span old borders. CNN, for example, beams its message worldwide; the Internet is global. By virtue of its dominance in communications, events in the United States have far flung consequences.

The issue of trust figured prominently in the FOCAS conversations as conferees worried that growing public cynicism toward media bodes ill for democracy. This line of discussion addressed several themes; one thread dealt with news content and another with industry concentration. Woven together, the argument suggests a vicious cycle in which the quality of public information accessible through the old media declines as media ownership consolidates.

If news—in a telling metaphor suggested by Westen—constitutes the "vitamins that keep a democracy healthy," the American corpus is badly undernourished. "Building trust is a vital part of the job the media has to do," explained John Oliver, publisher and CEO of the Afro-American Newspapers—that is, winning over the confidence of the estranged and disengaged. Of particular concern to Oliver are the youth in his Afro-American audience, enamoured of the antisocial elements of hip-hop, who must be convinced that there is a role for them in the political system." We have a lot of work to do," said Oliver," and I don't know if we can win."

The ability of the media to help reestablish faith in the democratic possibility is constrained when the information being disseminated tends not to address substantive issues but instead is trivial and diverting. "In this country we're operating under a huge 'trust deficiency,'" noted Pat Mitchell, president and CEO of the Public Broadcasting Service. "News is becoming entertainment, and the young population doesn't know the difference.

The audience only wants heroes and villains, not context or analysis. It's all about third-act screamfests, which don't help me function as a citizen." Others pursued this theme, suggesting that the media was guilty of "dumbing down" issues, of not covering complicated stories in sufficient depth. "I used to think reporters were lazy," noted Utah Governor Michael Leavitt, "that they were twenty-five-year-olds not prepared to deal with serious subjects." Increasingly, however, he has come to recognize the problem as one of the values of the industry rather than its personnel.

"News is interested only in features, crime, 'feel-good' or 'feel-bad' stories, not policy," noted Leavitt in explaining why journalists are reluctant to report on the substantive issues. Moreover, the consolidation of media is driving attention to national issues at the expense of local coverage that often has more immediate public impact.

Indeed, what has happened in the radio industry vividly illustrates how consolidation has drastically reduced the diversity of information. "Is media convergence good for democracy?" asked Marc Nathanson, vice chair of Charter Communications and chairman of the Broadcasting Board of Governors. "In fact, it has been very bad. Democracy was more robust in local media markets when there was diverse ownership of newspapers and radio."

In the acquisition frenzy unleashed by the 1996 Telecommunications Act—which lifted all ownership limits for radio broadcasters nationwide and allowed them to operate as many as eight signals in the country's largest markets—the industry has come to be dominated by a scant few mega broadcasters that saturate the country with standardized formats and announcers disguised to sound as if they originate locally.

With 1,200 stations, Clear Channel Communications is the dominant player, and, as Nathanson noted, "When Clear

Channel takes over a station, it often ephasizes more regional and national news." Is there an effective way to change this dynamic—to prompt leaders of conglomerates to take the democratic responsibilities of their media properties more seriously? "I'm not very optimistic," said Nathanson, "unless there is legislation or changes in the tax law to encourage it."

Patricia Hodgson, chief executive of Britain's Independent Television Commission, seconded the notion that the moment may have come to start thinking about intervening in media operations for the sake of the democratic imperative. "We have created these powerful media companies motivated by profit and popularity," Hodgson said. "We must ensure they give back that which supports our democracy."

Sentiment during the discussions was disinclined to view the electronic media with much hope. What has occurred with radio seems only too likely to occur similarly with television as pressure to relax ownership restrictions mounts. Even if present ownership arrangements endure, television is regarded with scant hope.

"At the beginning of television, it was taken for granted that it would actively promote democracy," noted Reed Hundt, former chairman of the FCC and senior advisor of McKinsey and Company. "That is no longer the case."

He went even further, concluding that "it's not at all clear that electronic media in the aggregate is a force that promotes democracy." Rather than offer diverse viewpoints, "what it does is promote widely spread opinions held simultaneously by large numbers of people."

These kinds of "wholesale" attitudes aren't the same thing as informed, reasoned beliefs individually arrived at that were understood to provide ballast to democracy.

Little in this argument is novel. The commercial media are organized to attract mass audiences that they sell, in turn, to advertisers. This model transforms the notion of "citizen" into that of "customer"—a dynamic that bears scant resemblance to any public purpose beyond commerce. "When you're running a TV network," observed Tracy Lawrence, president of Urban Television (UTV), "you're very clear that your goal is to get people to buy things." Drawing from personal experience as senior vice president and general manager of the Fox Family Channel, Lawrence said, "Your mission is to entertain. Judging from television, Americans are more concerned with acquiring a Jeep Wrangler than exercising their rights and responsibilities as citizens.

Consumerism has replaced democratic citizenship." The ongoing transformation of news into another form of mass media entertainment poses the threat of a "secular" change in the intellectual climate of the society. Idit Harel, chairman and CEO of MaMaMedia, questioned the fundamental values that are being invoked as the information climate becomes increasingly driven by commercial imperatives. "I believe that the main problem with current mass TV media is that it is in a bad loop of packaging and selling (to consumers and advertisers) news in journalistic formats loaded with negatives. Violent, trauma-generating content gets transmitted at the expense of content that suggests more positive, socially responsible experiences that could have uplifting and healing effects."

Invoking "values" raises the debate about information standards to another level of inquiry. The conventional complaint about commercial media is that it "dumbs down" the news, rendering the public less qualified to exercise political responsibilities. As Harel's remarks suggest, the essential fabric of social bonds themselves may be jeopardized by the media's excessive attention to the public as "consumers" (defined by private interests) rather than "citizens" (possessed of a common purpose). "The values expressed in much of the programming and packaging of both news and entertainment is not positive nor productive for democracy, " said Harel.

THE DISAPPEARING ELECTORATE AND THE MEDIA

The lynchpin of democracy is elections. Although few people would suggest that the media singularly determines voter turnout, the media play a critical role in energizing the electorate. The measure of so much of the media critique voiced during the conference sessions is the growing number of people who do not exercise their franchise to vote—a condition that is particularly acute with youth. As shown in a study conducted jointly by The Washington Post, the Henry J.Kaiser Family Foundation, and Harvard University, the majority of voters under age thirty do not vote; a mere 23 percent of all twenty-five-year-olds go to the polls. In light of these trends, there is reason to indict media performance.

The 2002 election cycle provided a stark example of how the industry's priorities affected coverage. Television newscasts in the largest 50 media markets ran four times as many political commercials as campaign stories. ("Many station managers feel that putting political news on their air waves would be ratings poison," noted one of the directors of the Washington Post study.)

This imbalance—with paid commercials so dramatically overshadowing objective reporting—effectively "monetizes" what democratic theory idealizes as the media's considerably more disinterested role in the process of shaping public opinion. Several conferees even wondered aloud whether by acting in this fashion the media as currently configured is, in effect, an "enemy of democracy."

> *"I've been a finance chairman and a candidate," observed Gaston Caperton, president and CEO of the College Board and former governor of West Virginia, "and I can tell you there's a whole lot more value by a candidate being in conversation with real people in communities than in being in cocktail parties collecting checks." The underlying problem is the orientation of the industry. "Around election time conversations in the boardrooms of media companies don't routinely discuss how to improve the news coverage," noted Caperton. "Rather, they talk about sales and the big influx of advertising revenues that can be expected with tight races."*

When television journalists do a story, the kind of issues they choose to address also figures prominently in the criticism of the media. At a subtle level of manipulation, content is captive to the will of the political parties, with reporters taking the cue for their agenda through prompts from the professional politicians.

> *"The news media is complicit in focusing on the issues that the parties choose to focus on," argues William Kennard, former FCC chairman and managing director of telecommunications and media at the Carlyle Group. "Many issues that ordinary people care about don't figure in the discourse, and the media ends up disenfranchising those people from the debate. Issues that the parties don't want to discuss, or that aren't in the broadcast industry's interest, get swept aside."*

THE DEMOCRATIC OPPORTUNITY OF NEW MEDIA

If the old media is suspect with respect to its ability to promote democracy, the new media remain untested and largely a blank slate. Several advocates have heralded the

Internet and other new media as harbingers of a new age of democratic flowering. Before celebrating this potential, it is instructive to recall Reed Hundt's cautionary tale of the hope with which television originally was viewed and its ultimate failure to deliver on that promise. Nevertheless, there is reason to hope that the Internet—as an extended metaphor for high-density, individually addressed, packet-switched digital information—may well energize the political process.

Later in this discussion we consider some specific technological and economic issues pertaining to the new media's political impact. For the moment, however, the general argument made by John Clippinger, chairman of Parity, Inc., frames the parameters of possibility. Drawing an analogy from system architecture, Clippinger likened the problem of "trust" in the political system to "robustness" in a network. "Trust comes out of transparency," Clippinger pointed out, likening democracy to peer-to-peer computing.

The more transparent a network is, the less its operations are hidden and inaccessible, the more it is robust, responsive, and likely to maximize the fullest potential of its users. He cited the enormous success of eBay as a prime example of the potential that resides in transparent new media. "When notions of accountability and transparency are absent, on the other hand, when a system seems rigidly structured and controlled by 'unseen forces' in which disproportionate power is vested, people withdraw from the network."

In predicting whether the new media will support or undermine democracy, whether they will be more or less capable of inspiring in their users a trust in the integrity of the political system, Clippinger suggests that one look at how they function. One model could turn out to be authoritarian rather than liberating in nature, dominated by "dedicated point-to-point circuit architecture." The other—

more comforting from a democratic perspective—would be networks operating under "distributed control where there is no single party in control." (This is how the Internet currently functions, although subject to future change through technical design, regulatory action, or commercial forces).

Clippinger's argument suggests that new media, regardless of content, are not politically neutral but are more or less disposed to democracy depending on their system architecture. Distributed control, observed Clippinger, is analogous to what the Greeks discovered when they invented democracy: "You take your identity from being in a group; that's who you are. When you lose that sense of who you are, you become disaffected."

Old media or new, the stakes are high. The tenets of democracy are predicated on the fundamental presumption that the citizenry cares about how it is governed, that they desire information about public affairs, that they have access to such information, that they feel allegiance to the commonwealth, and that they vote. Although institutional checks-and-balances can rein in the threat of tyranny from the state, there is also the danger that the legitimacy of the government can be eroded from below by a passive population.

When the conditions of citizen engagement are not being met—when they neither want nor receive relevant information, when they are indifferent to voting—the likelihood of this "hollowing out" of democracy grows.

Unlike earlier ages, ours is an era in which the challenge facing social engineers is not too little communication capability but perhaps too much. An abundance of information is a mixed blessing. With a multitude of voices screaming to be recognized—some louder than others because they are better financed—it becomes harder to distinguish messages with value from those that are extraneous or blatantly self-serving.

Mental switchboards are overloaded. Rather than render meaning, hyperactive media ecology evokes confusion, and one must wonder how long democracy can prosper in such an environment.

"Attention," Charles Firestone, executive director of the Aspen Institute's Communications and Society Program, observed, "has become the scarce commodity." The challenge facing policymakers is to devise appropriate responses to recalibrate the balance between the potential to make information available and its capacity to enhance the exercise of democratic citizenship so that the media, in terms consistent with Tracy Westen's model, can again undergird and not undercut democracy.

THE EVOLVING MEDIA CONTEXT AND THE PROSPECTS FOR CHANGE

The future impact of cyberspace on politics remains to be seen; for the moment the influence of commercial media remains unrivaled. Throughout the conversations in Aspen there were references to the power the media possesses to dominate discourse and to define agendas. Although the media may claim to be merely messengers delivering somebody else's messages, the issues they choose to address significantly shape public opinion. Tracy Westen cited some reasons why the media occupy such a singular status: "They are independently powerful, they sit astride the information that comes into the home, and they are particularly important in influencing what happens in their local communities."

Concerns about the disproportionate power exercised by the media in a democracy become more compelling as the industry itself becomes more concentrated. If there are fewer independent media organizations, is it not logical to expect a corresponding decrease in the diversity of different points of view? Moreover, will this situation not become more aggravated as communication technology converges, enabling single companies to control the distribution of information along a variety of channels? These "macro" questions constituted the subtext for consideration of whether there is reasonable basis for believing that the tilt of the media can be shifted to give more impetus to dynamics that promote democracy.

MEDIA CONCENTRATION

The map of the media landscape was redrawn during the 1990s through consolidation (as discussed above in reference to radio). Anecdotally one can cite waves of mergers that resulted in the disappearance of established companies and conflated management within new conglomerates.

With regard to concentration, however, Eli Noam, director of the Columbia University Institute for Tele-Information, has observed that "views are strong but numbers are scarce. Most people actually do believe strongly that the media is more concentrated than it used to be, but I would suggest that the question is much more open than that." In testimony before the Senate Commerce Committee, Noam cited trends in the classic media industries for the period from 1986 to 1998 that paint a mixed picture of concentration.

The weighted average of four-firm market share for the mass media industries rose from 33 percent in 1986 to 40 percent in 1998. For the three major television networks, it declined from 70 percent to 53 percent. For local television stations, the top four firms' share rose nationally from 15 percent to 26 percent. For cable television distribution, it rose from 37 percent to 60 percent. Concentration more than doubled in radio station ownership and book publishing.

The national movie theater, newspaper, and magazine markets remained relatively unconcentrated, with the top four firms accounting for-one-quarter of sales.

Where Noam did see unmistakable evidence of concentration was at the local level with respect to newspapers, cable television, and telecommunication. "It cannot be said that U.S. media have become, in general, more concentrated," Noam concluded. "Some segments have, others have become less concentrated." In sum, there is no problem as measured by Justice Department antitrust standards.

Noam's picture of the media landscape offers relative comfort for those who fear the contraction of diversity. "Media today is more concentrated than four or five years ago but less so than twenty years ago," he observed at the FOCAS session. "We don't see a huge danger in concentration or convergence in 'wall-to-wall' companies that control everything. If you think about it, the telecom companies are not really mass media. The mass media companies are not doing IT [information technology] stuff. IT companies don't do much of mass media."

Without disputing Noam's research, however, there is an intuitive sense among many observers that the current organization of the media industry, even if not formally concentrated in antitrust terms, operates with fewer diverse outlets than in the past.

In a recent broadcast, Bill Moyers staked out this position, describing how powerful the reigning media corporations have become and, by implication, the grip they have on the public's access to information: "Twenty-five years ago there were fifty owners of America's major media outlets. Now there are six. Two-thirds of today's newspaper markets are monopolies. Over half the radio audience is controlled by four corporations."

FAILURE TO REALIZE "SYNERGY"

The business rationale for much of the merger initiative was "synergy": the notion that digital technology would render the content of different media so compatible that they are destined to converge so that a company can profit from "cross-purposing"—say, its own movie production and book publishing for Internet distribution via its own cable system. In retrospect, synergy may have been more a Wall Street mantra than a sound operational tactic. As the likes of Viacom, Bertelsmann, and Vivendi announced acquisition after acquisition, however, the strategy gained credibility.

In the intervening years, the anticipated benefits from these megaconglomerates have been slow to appear. This fact doesn't surprise Noam, who observed that the broadband explosion, long anticipated as the route to synergy, consistently fails to occur. "I've been kind of looking at this area for easily twenty years, and broadband is always going to happen two years from now—and it's been like that for twenty years."

That there is little evidence that synergy works as a business principle doesn't surprise those who worked in media companies charged with implementing the strategy. Pat Mitchell, in her former role as president of CNN Production and Time, Inc.

Television, was charged with finding synergistic collaborations with Time, Inc. properties—magazines and books. She recalled arriving at the first meeting of the heads of the different business units "quite excited about the enormous, rich, deep content which was now possible to aggregate with some sort of impact on citizens." Instead, she reported, the conversation turned entirely to the question of contact with consumers and how to market to each other's customers as a kind of captive audience. "It didn't turn out to be an approach that worked," Mitchell said, "but it was the strategy that drove the thinking." Randy Blotky, chairman and CEO of Technology Convergence Partners, also had been at AOL Time Warner and saw first-hand how "synergy" operated. Much of his focus within AOL Time Warner was "to create constructs for businesses that were consumer centric." The model that informed his approach seemed a natural outgrowth of the traditional role that media plays as a "trusted agent" of the public. "The Internet acts as the enabling 'grid' on which someone or something becomes the trusted agent for a broad segment of its constituency," Blotky said.

"At AOL Time Warner we were trying to figure out what that constituency wanted from this medium, when they wanted it, and the price they were willing to pay for it in order to achieve that 'accepted agent' status. In some cases, by the way, the payment turns out to be zero, but not always—and the real point was that once 'trusted agent' status was achieved, your brand can live in the hearts and minds of that constituency virtually in perpetuity." Drawing from this experience, Blotky came to realize that "convergence is like the blind man and the elephant: It can mean a lot of different things to different people, depending on their perspective."

William Kennard, as FCC chairman, was charged with regulatory responsibility for these companies during the acquisition fervour; in this role, he heard media executives making the case for convergence.

"It was like listening to teenagers talk about sex. Everybody thinks everybody else is doing it, when in fact very few people are actually doing it. And those who are doing it are not doing it very well. But nevertheless, everybody thinks that when they finally do it, it will be really great." Looking back on the mergers he approved, he now admits that "the benefits were oversold to regulators and the market. People were anticipating efficiencies of merging content and delivery that haven't been realized."

To be fair, these benefits may still come. Technologists point to a near-future when every laptop will be a network communicator, with integration at the chip level for wireless local area network (LAN) capability. The "coming" of broadband may become an established fact, bringing in its wake new varieties of content—including some devoted to advancing the democratic agenda. Zoë Baird, president of the Markle Foundation, spoke about this possibility: "I think it is incumbent on us who care very deeply about the continuation of innovation in the development of information to help throw out possible business models that might lead to success that also preserves the values we care about."

Baird recalled a conversation with Gerald Levin, when he was chairman of AOL Time Warner, in which he said, "If you can just focus on the economics of the media as it develops going forward and help us figure out a way that we can make money and still serve all the public interests you care about, that would be the single most important thing you could do."

On the other hand are those who are less sanguine about the implications of consolidation. "Technological convergence leads to financial convergence," observes Reed Hundt, who presided at the FCC during the passage of the landmark 1996 Telecommunications Act. "We've thought for over 100 years that it was good to have different media compete with each other and have technologies compete with each other. From a democratic perspective, multiple media in a community build different sources of support." Indeed, Bill Clinton would have vetoed the Telecommunications Act if it had included an amendment allowing newspapers and television stations to merge in a single city.

The principle of having different media have different voices of communication appears to be very much in jeopardy, however. The regulatory environment is not favorably disposed to erecting firewalls between existing media. Meanwhile, the collapse of the stock market and private equity sources means that there is scant funding for those who would build new modes of information delivery.

GATEKEEPERS AND BOTTLENECKS

What is left in the aftermath of the 1990s media megamergers is an emerging communication "network of networks" in which, critics point out, there are fewer and fewer gatekeepers deciding who gains entry. "The problem with diversity is where bottlenecks come up," notes Peter Price, president of the National Academy of Television Arts and Sciences, citing cable television. "There is immense consolidation in the cable industry, which is the lead pipe for broadband.

How do you structure a situation where you avoid monopolies doing the things that monopolies do naturally? You want to be cautious about policies that appear to produce good results but are really a way for monopolists to deflect government control."

One of the things the cable bottleneck constricts is programming. Cable promotes itself with images of technological abundance, suggesting a limitless array of options targeted to specialized audiences. In fact, however, space on the tuner is precious real estate (particularly on the basic, nonpremium tier), parcelled out by the operating companies as a scarce commodity from which they seek to derive maximum advantage. In the early days of cable, when there were multiple operators with expansive demand for product, programmers were in a reasonably fair competitive position. The wave of consolidation, however, has significantly restricted their universe of buyers, to the detriment of content diversity.

In seeking to launch an independent programming service aimed at the multicultural urban population, Tracy Lawrence of UTV has encountered problems that were not a factor earlier in her career, when she participated in the launch of cable channels. "It would seem like it should be a 'no brainer' for operators to look for a channel that would capture what's happening in urban culture," she assumed, "but it's a very different process now."

To get venture capital, it is necessary to have advance commitment that the service will be carried by enough local cable systems to reach a suitable national audience. The way the industry is now configured, there are only two companies in a position to make such an assurance. "Launching a new channel means conversations effectively with two people," Lawrence observed. "It's not about the idea anymore. It's about who you know, where you've been, what big names you can associate with your channel."

Similar bottlenecks exist in other information industries in which a handful of major players dominate the production and distribution of content. Even the Internet—which one might intuitively expect to be the most competitive of media—is experiencing consolidation. Indeed, according to Eli Noam, the notion that it remains "wide open" is false. "The industry that is increasing its concentration most rapidly is Internet service provision. If the trend line continues on the backbone level and ISP level, it will be more concentrated than any other."

William Kennard also pointed out the dampening effect bottlenecks can have on programming options. New business models, regardless of their commercial potential, can be prematurely extinguished if only a few companies control access to the market.

"I am absolutely convinced that we will come up with better business models if we create an environment where more people get access to the end user, and you break down the gatekeeper situation. Those models are not going to come necessarily from the strategic corporate planners in the big companies when it's not in their interest to do so."

WHY CLASSIC ANTITRUST DOESN'T APPLY TO MEDIA

A conventional response to trade restraints in the past has been governmental regulation, but in the case of the media and information businesses, even advocates of diversity are reluctant to recommend this option. Antitrust law as a tool was not designed to promote the democratic value of diverse discourse, and it would be difficult to develop appropriate standards to gauge desirable levels of competition in a business that is unlike virtually any other in terms of the unique importance it plays in the political life of the society. Classic criteria of competition employ economic measures, not subjective considerations such as "the people's need to know."

In an analysis prepared for this discussion, Reed Hundt summarized the inapplicability of antitrust law in this context: Antitrust law is concerned solely with the goal of efficiency. Its purpose is to make sure that markets are competitive, so that they maximize output from productive capability. There are at least two reasons why antitrust law alone is an inadequate paradigm for determining how many broadcasters or newspapers or any media outlet we might wish in order to perpetuate our democracy, entertain ourselves, grow our economy, or provide outlets for creative energy.

First, the antitrust law necessarily focuses on the buying or selling of product or services; that is what a market comprises. But the dissemination, for example, of political news for free does not necessarily come from nor should it be gated by the profit motive, or the pricing of media content.

We might simply want political news to be broadly and freely given away, and under those circumstances it is difficult to see how a competitive or a noncompetitive market for media content or advertising time will further that goal. Indeed, the more competitive the media market, it is possible, even plausible, that the more likely it will be that the media outlets would be disinclined to afford free time for political news.

Second, antitrust law can conclude that a market is reasonably competitive even if it has only one or two or three competitors. That is because other considerations are relevant, such as ease of entry or the efficiency of a natural monopoly. In particular, Chicago-school antitrust thinkers over the last thirty years have espoused a certain degree of government tolerance for such highly concentrated markets. Yet while the antitrust law might tolerate such concentrated markets, it seems plain that the risk to democracy of having only a few, or indeed just one, speaker or outlet for speech in a media market would be quite substantial. The parallel with totalitarian societies should be resisted, yet it is noteworthy that we reject in many other circumstances any sympathy with societies that limited or monopolized media.

Moreover, antitrust law will almost always conclude that markets with five competitors are competitive, provided that no one has price-setting market share. Yet from the perspective of forming an inclusive, diverse democracy, we might well conclude that we need at least six, or seven, or some such higher number of outlets. An example is the persistent if intermittent effort by government to create outlets for different language, or for media owned by women or minorities or small businesses. Such outlets might be sixth, or seventh, or eighth entrants in media markets; antitrust law might not regard them as necessary to create competition, but for other reasons we might value them very highly.

Despite the consensus about the limitations of regulatory theory, support remains for maintaining at least a semblance of the competitive framework that has evolved over the past decades. The decision by the FCC to initiate a reconsideration of longstanding ownership rules is certain to produce political cross-currents.

On one hand are those who advocate wiping the slate clean and taking the government out of the business of monitoring the communications industry, on the other those who are unwilling to abandon the principle that diversity is best served by more rather than fewer owners of media. Kevin Martin, a sitting FCC commissioner, suggested alternative ways that criteria could be framed to address the need for diversity while only minimally interfering with the free operations of the market.

The traditional approach to assure competition in each specific medium may be obsolete, Martin opined, in an era when the same services can be obtained from a variety of sources. "If content is not exclusive to any particular content provider, then when you say there need to be multiple intermediaries, one of the questions I would have is, do you really need multiple intermediaries within each distribution platform? Or is it just that there need to be multiple distributors of that information?

That gets to the point of open access to service providers. If you have several satellite providers, cable providers, and telephone providers all providing broadband internet access service, do you actually need access to each multiple facility, or is it enough to have 'across-the-board' access? That's one of the crucial issues the Commission is facing: how much of access has to do with platform competition."

> *"We have to be careful not to confuse open access to information with open access to service providers," Martin cautioned. "Maybe we need to have a certain number of access providers to make sure service is being offered at a competitive price and in a competitive manner, but it doesn't have to be infinite to be in the consumer's best interest."*

Given the bias toward relaxing rules, regulation does not appear to be the most likely way to unclog media bottlenecks. A more viable solution would appear to lie with Zoë Baird's enthusiasm for the development of new business models that are capable of serving the public interest and sustaining themselves commercially. It may well prove to be in this arena—helping such emerging enterprises by protecting their viability during a critical incubation period—that the FCC and other governmental agencies may operate in the future under the auspices of a new formulation of competition along the lines that Martin suggests.

This subject is discussed later, but for the moment it is worth remembering that in the zeal to liberate communication initiatives that have been held back by archaic rules we not lose sight of the positive consequences that can result from enlightened regulation formulated under a different paradigm than classic antitrust.

NURTURING NEW MARKET NICHES

A cause for optimism in the prospects of new content business models is the growing likelihood that the returns on investment of the concentrated media companies will prove less than promised, and they are too unwieldy to stay intact. Anecdotally we already have seen signs of trouble. Vivendi and Bertelsmann have dismissed the CEO architects of their acquisition strategies; AOL trades at a fraction of its value when it acquired Time Warner; AT&T's costly entry into cable now-appears misguided. "If the question is 'are these companies inherently unstable?' the answer is 'yes,'" concluded Eli Noam. "The present downturn related to consolidation shows the inherent instability of the media/ telecom companies."

For the media giants, the "old way" to make money through market concentration may have reached a point of diminishing returns. If these companies are forced to divest pieces of themselves to improve their balance sheets, niches of opportunity will arise. "We're still in a period where we don't know what the business models are that will be successful," noted Zoë Baird.

Providing offerings that better integrate people living in the same local market also was considered worthy of exploration. "The media have been leading a movement away from localism and much more toward nationalism and globalism," noted Marc Nathanson of Charter Communications. "After we brought cable into Kingsport, Tennessee, for example, kids started dressing the same way in Kingsport as in New York City." To some observers, this muting of local culture and regional distinctiveness is a factor in the decline of community and impedes democratic discourse.

Another category of opportunity lies on the content side, with interactive offerings that engage audiences in a participatory way that builds democratic attitudes and behaviours among users and contributes to the growth of democratic communities.

Kids' relationships with media have changed with successive generations, creating new openings for innovative business models. Idit Harel of MaMaMedia offers a compelling taxonomy to describe these generational divides, based on their experiences with media as they were growing up: Baby Boomers as kids learned how to "consume" media passively; Generation X learned to be a bit more active and "choose" their media experiences—initially by way of the remote control, then through television programming such as Sesame Street and Nickelodeon that inculcate an attitude within the targeted audience that "you have to be mindful when you view this TV show (Sesame Street), and you have the power to select this channel rather then a channel for parents (Nickelodeon), it's us versus them"; Clickerati, the current generation that is coming of age, growing up with television, cable, and the Internet, learn from a very young age how to "consume, choose, and create" (they want not just to receive media but to make their own; they seek "tools and not answers").

> *"The medium," Harel says, playing off Marshall McLuhan's famous axiom, "is no longer the message. It's what you do with it, the activity, that matters. Content is better if it can be consumed as well as constructed, received as well as personalized. It's not about high tech for this computer-skilled generation, it's about 'my tech.'"*

In Harel's view, this active participation in media experiences can contribute to growing more active people in general. The new content product agenda, again to quote one of her pithy aphorisms, focuses on "the Three X's: eXploration, eXpression, eXchange"—not just on show and instruct or entertain.

In addition to making the media experience more democratic in this sense, a democratic political content site or online channel for kids, for example, would be about providing a conduit to other people's content: articles, games, information, news, polls and surveys and enabling users to create and circulate their own.

As a means to encourage children to expand their universes and thus become more receptive to being socialized to democracy, the Internet appears to be a powerful tool. Although it might be expected that Internet usage would encourage social isolation among children, in fact just the opposite is the case. Referring to research done at the UCLA Communications Policy Centre, Marc Nathanson pointed out that "the children who spend more time on the internet are more social, less isolated, and this is throughout the world, not just in the United States."

POLICY APPROACHES TO INCUBATING NEW MEDIA MODELS

The swirl of shifting commercial and political forces buffeting media as it steadily digitizes poses serious quandaries to those charged with overseeing communications policy. Whereas the essence of the traditional regulatory approach is removing barriers to entry and maintaining competition, that may no longer suffice as a raison d'etre in the present context. If the media industries, as Eli Noam believes, are destined to be increasingly cyclical, policy also must adjust to quickly changing circumstances and itself adapt a more cyclical approach. Permanent solutions cease to be feasible in such a fluid context. Instead, as Noam describes, the government will have to "mix and match" among three general policy options:

- "Laissez-faire, let it rip";
- Accommodations with convergence through "side deals" such as those long maintained with AT&T and the three major television networks ("we'll give you an oligopoly, but you'll have to serve the public interest"); and
- Prohibition of oligopoly by special concessions and collaboration formulas designed to keep competitors

alive, with the Newspaper Preservation Act serving as one model.

Aligning new business development and implementation with regulatory policy constitutes a preeminent challenge to those who would seek to reform the media for the sake of the democratic commonwealth. Beyond the historic ways this goal has been approached, social thinkers are beginning to propose a new concept that is especially applicable to the digital age—the commons. One way to do align the public and private sectors is to create communication business initiatives supported by government rules that act, in the words of one advocate, to "reclaim the commons," which he powerfully defines as that "vast range of resources that the American people collectively own, but which are rapidly being enclosed: privatized, traded in the market, and abused."

REDEFINING THE GROUND RULES

To restate the argument thus far, consolidation of media entities over the past decade has produced a more restricted flow in the variety and sources of information, particularly public-spirited information of the kind that is critical to the exercise of citizenship in a democracy.

Gary Knell, president and CEO of the Sesame Workshop that produces Sesame Street, summed up the constraints imposed by bottlenecks when he observed, at a previous FOCAS gathering, that "distribution is king": "You've got to have great content, but if you don't have distribution—if you're not partnered up with a Viacom or an AOL Time Warner—it is very tough to get your content out there."

Although there are countless similar anecdotal observations, it is problematic whether current media concentration contravenes current antitrust standards of restraint of trade. Moreover, the spirit of regulation since the 1996 Telecommunications Act has been, effectively, to give more rather than less freedom to markets, so the climate is ill-disposed to a wave of assertive rule-making. Yet as PBS's Pat Mitchell pointedly asks, "What happened to the concept of the public's entitlement or ownership of these distribution pipes or spectrum?"

The Internet constitutes a wild card in the mix, a medium virtually unknown only a decade ago that now is transforming various forms of communications. If the Internet is left undefended from market forces, advocates for the free flow of information fear that ISPs, portal companies, and information aggregators such as Google.com will erect proprietary "walled gardens" around content, imposing de facto tariffs on the traffic of ideas.

By embedding these gatekeeping functions in hidden code, making it impossible hypothetically to access, say, The New York Times with a Microsoft browser or websites that are not specially tagged, the public may not even be aware that its universe of information is circumscribed. On the other hand, if the Internet is protected as a neutral terrain with universal access to content, it could prove to be a forceful instrument of the public interest.

Statutes and rules will figure prominently in determining which way the Internet goes. A rationale for activism that is different from current standards of antitrust would make the case more compelling for administrative oversight of the Internet.

As distinguished legal scholar Cass Sunstein points out, few issues are more important to democracy than an informed electorate, yet scant concern is directed to how the requisite information is to be made available.

"The informed citizen plays an important role in democracy theory," Sunstein wrote in Republic.com; "the communication systems supposed to supply the citizens with political information have received little attention." A more robust theory that addresses the public mandate to nurture these communication systems is needed—one that shifts critical tests away from economic consequences on consumers and to the democratic impact on citizens.

PRESERVING THE "INNOVATIVE COMMONS" ON THE INTERNET

A fruitful vein that is worth exploring in this context is the concept of the "social commons." Lawrence Lessig writes probingly on this subject in The Future of Ideas. Simply put, Lessig challenges the "taken-for granted" premise that "progress always comes from dividing resources among private owners."

He argues, without being "anti-property," that there are instances in which maximum innovation and social benefit result from an asset that is, in effect, "nonowned." Lessig is not pitting state against market but "free" against "controlled." "That war is over. For most resources, most of the time, the market trumps the state." The roads are free in this sense when drivers can use them at will, parks are free, "equations developed by Kepler and Newton and modified by Einstein are free to scientists plotting an orbit of a spacecraft."

Where there is a benefit from leaving a resource free, and where it is not diluted by overconsumption or underdeveloped because of inadequate incentives, Lessig argues that the public interest falls under neither private nor state control. ("It is an iron law of modern democracy that when you create a regulator, you create a target for influence, and when you create a target for influence, those in the best position to influence will train their efforts upon that target.") For most of its life to date, the Internet has been just such an "innovation commons" in Lessig's terms.

True, the wires and computers it runs on are owned, and much of the content is owned, but the "code" that moves digital bits freely through the system from end to end—the essence of what makes the Internet such an awesome communication medium—is free.

That code is open and accessible to all, neutral and nondiscriminatory in its operation, the possession of everybody and nobody. Lessig's fear, shared by many of the conferees at the FOCAS session, is that this freedom is likely to be short-lived. The agenda of the media conglomerates is to grow revenue by "monetizing" their capabilities into profitable commercial products. As they enter into the Internet space, it is natural for them to look for ways to monetize their leverage over the system itself.

The reason much of the content and community on the Internet currently bodes well for democracy is, as William Kennard points out, "the public access through open platforms." It is not necessarily in the perceived interest of the network providers, however, to continue to provide these open platforms. The leverage Microsoft exerts on software developers to accommodate their products to the "closed" platform of Windows operating systems suggests what could happen if the Internet platform were to become similarly proprietary. If such a world comes to pass, predicted Kennard, the Internet environment would resemble the situation in the software development environment: "Business models become binary—either find a niche where Microsoft can't come after you or sell to Microsoft and that's your exit."

Patricia Hodgson, of Britain's Independent Television Commission, recounted how the United Kingdom faced an analogous situation: The entire satellite broadcast platform was controlled by one company, which was understandably reluctant to open its set-top box to other services. It was eventually persuaded to do so. "Now the most interesting thing about that is that as a result we see on TV all sorts of competitors were up there. It makes the satellite company money because their packages are richer than they would otherwise be.

They are so pleased with what has happened that they now boast that they introduced open broadcasting to the UK. Now the same challenge is to obtain the same thing for the broadband bottleneck into the home, to provide capability to interconnect any-to-any as in plain old telephony."

THE THREAT TO OPEN ACCESS

The possibility that browsers will cease to be neutral navigators of the web but instead will be subtly coded to favour or ignore sites struck the conferees as particularly ominous. As a medium that is "pull" rather than "push," the Internet enables the user to seek information from a virtually limitless reservoir (unlike broadcast, where finite content is pumped out, or pushed, to an essentially passive user)—but this limitlessness is contingent on the effectiveness of searching capability.

Kevin Hess, vice president for federal affairs of TDS Telecom, noted, for example, that the wiring of schools and libraries has significantly added to the ability of children to get answers to specific inquiries. "My daughter did not realize that everyone does not vote in elections," Hess said.

If a pull medium is to function effectively, the capacity to search its knowledge base becomes critical. "The value proposition," foresees John Clippinger of Parity, Inc., "is not going to be in selling content but in creating the context by which people get access.

There is a revenue model in the ability to tag things and find them." On the other hand, monetizing this aggregator function could create an Internet dominated by webmasters deploying sophisticated user information embedded in profiles to tag sites. If this became the standard, it would contradict the principles of the open commons. Such practices could easily transform "pull" into "entrapment."

If market forces are given free rein, it is reasonable to worry that the Internet might follow a course that jeopardizes the commons. "The business model of the new media companies is to throw millions of dollars on marketing their solution and bringing customers to their product through whatever technology they're pushing," cautioned Peter Price of the National Academy of Television Arts and Sciences.

"This first wave of Internet technology makes for a proliferation of voices. The second wave of technology, broadband, suddenly works against proliferation because there are fewer gatekeepers." One can only surmise what will happen in a third and fourth generation of technology as gates keep narrowing, increasingly moving into the realm of search engines.

An architecture whereby each application must "register" itself with the network could undermine open networks. The network could be designed in advance so that only certain kinds of applications could run on it. A pricing system could be built into the system to control how the network is used. All such acts of concentration "direct the future," in Lessig's scheme, giving the concentrators the power to steer evolution as it benefits them.

The future, Lessig fears, may already be cast. In his opinion, two companies, AOL Time Warner and Microsoft—neither of which has committed itself to a neutral and open platform—will effectively define the next phase of the Internet's life. "Additions that benefit either company will be encouraged; additions that don't, won't. Content and access will once again be controlled; the innovation commons will have been carved up and sold."

Needless to say, "carving up and selling" of the Internet innovation commons would strike a harsh blow to its capacity to contribute to democratic discourse. As broadcasters have aptly demonstrated, in the absence of rigorous requirements there is little reason to expect commercial media entities to devote much of their resources to substantive non-entertainment programming.

To surrender the Internet—and its potential to extend the democratic process—without a fight is unworthy of those who would contend for its promise. Advocates of "public goods philosophy"—a variation on the theme of the commons—propose remedies. On the other side of the Atlantic, the agenda seems clear.

> *"The unrestrained market will not produce either the range or quality of broadcasting or the full range of Internet sites that is desirable and which the new technology makes possible," concludes Andrew Graham, an English economist, in his study Public Policy Issues for UK Broadcasting. "For this we need a thoughtfully designed broadcasting policy in which the public and the private and the global and the local sectors complement one another."*

Although more skeptical about the eventual outcome, Lessig frames the issue with equal clarity. "If the original Internet architected an innovation space that was free, if it built that space by creating an environment where innovations would not be checked, if it was defined by a code layer that was open, then as the Internet moves onto fat pipes, will the same principle govern the code layer of the Net? Will broadband respect the principle of end-to-end as narrowband has? And if it doesn't, will the government do anything to resist the change?"

Therein lies the critical question: Will the government do anything? What is required is reasonably simple to define:

The government should encourage adherence to open code and prohibit any of the major players from architecting the Internet space to serve their own strategic purposes at the expense of the commons. Enacting this stance as national policy would go a long way toward securing the democratic foundations of this most comprehensive communication medium.

CONCLUSION

For democracy to flourish, its citizens require information, ideas, and opinions about matters of public import. A system wherein sovereignty resides with the people cannot long be sustained by an uninformed public. The classic source of such information, ideas, and opinions has been the media. Indeed, it is to serve as a trustworthy source free of fear or favour that the First Amendment protects them. FOCAS participants expressed concern, however, that the quality of public affairs reporting by the media routinely fails to further the democratic cause.

The concentration of the industry into a handful of multimedia conglomerates for which news is something of an ancillary mission does not help the situation. Nor does the FCC's recent abandonment of behavioural rules requiring a standard of public service from broadcasters.

At the same time—perhaps the cause of media neglect or perhaps the result—fewer and fewer people consider themselves politically engaged or even vote in elections. The growing indifference of the electorate, most notably among those under thirty years old, would seem to undermine long-term democratic prospects. Lynda Resnick, co-owner and vice chairman of Roll International, expressed the underlying concern that animated much of the conversation. Discussing why a growing portion of the population (especially youth) seems not to care about exercising civic responsibilities, she discounted the idea that traditional media fare could change their behaviour.

Drawing on her marketing background, Resnick was skeptical about trying to "force-feed democracy." Instead, she recommended "finding out what people are open to" and embedding democratic messages within. "What we need is a better idea about how to stimulate them." An example of a "big media idea" currently being tested by the Voice of America (VOA) to ignite democratic sentiment among Middle Eastern youth was described by Marc Nathanson and a colleague on the Broadcasting Board of Governors, Tom Korologos. Instead of all-talk cerebral fare, the VOA is experimenting with a pop music format modelled on the American Top-100 FM style.

Broadcast in Arabic, interspersing American songs with songs in Arabic, the goal of Radio Sawa (which means "together") is to attract listeners for the news segments sandwiched into the music. In a matter of months the service has acquired a sizeable audience, and though it is too early to predict the results, the least that can be said is that its listeners are hearing balanced regional news regularly and receiving a less biased portrait of the United States than they receive on state-sponsored media. Indeed, as Eli Noam noted, "American popular culture may not be the hook but rather the 'meaning' itself. The way it portrays the American lifestyle—how women are portrayed, the legal system, the police—is advertisement for democracy."

Although none of the conferees suggested that such an approach be tried here (for one reason, federal law prohibits the VOA from broadcasting domestically), Radio Sawa is a provocative example of how media can be deployed to stimulate exposure to public affairs. When the FCC employed behaviour solutions, stations had to provide news. Now other methods must be tried.

Tax breaks for stations that offer public affairs material were recommended as a possibility. Many of the group were positively disposed to the idea that commercial users of the broadcast spectrum should be taxed or charged a license fee that would be used to sustain public service media. Another recommendation was that commercial stations be encouraged to air specially produced public interest insert spots. The specific recommendations are less important at this point than the need to stimulate thinking about new possibilities to expand the capacity of the media to promote democracy.

Meanwhile, the Internet—the "medium of media"—looms over the landscape of the future. Arguably the single most important communications issue to be decided in the near future is whether conditions of freedom or control will prevail. If the answer is freedom—if the Internet is to function with open code and end-to-end intelligence—the opportunities to devise ways to stimulate democracy will be limited only by our imagination and desire. If, on the other hand, the answer is control—if the companies that own the pipes get to own the code—commercial values are likely to prevail over democratic ones.

9

POLITICS AND JOURNALISM AS SPECTACLE

The ideal of journalism is that reporters serve the public interest by pressing the powerful - political, commercial, social, religious - to explain themselves and justify their decisions which affect the rest of society. The reality of journalism is that reporters are part of the class of powerful and tend to serve their interests.

In Culture Industry, Heinz Steinert writes:

> *Representing politics in democracy involves press releases and press conferences, as well as all the other forms of political announcement that take place via the journalistic apparatus. Only occasionally does anyone ever ask a question that is not entirely predictable or that has not been 'cleared' beforehand, and when they do, it usually happens in the course of an interview or a political talk-show. In order to make politics look exciting and dramatic, political activity has to be represented in a way that takes in conflicts and controversies, plans and counterinitiatives, schemes and struggles to implement them.*

Political journalists have become 'insiders', and they are treated as a kind of courtly entourage. They are invited to all the important events, and have themselves turned into politicians. Journalists are political players, for they have power over a particular resource. They control access to an audience, and the size of this audience determines the extent of their power (just as it does in other types of advertising).

Journalism is part of a media culture where everything is turned into entertainment of some sort, so it's not surprising that "spectacle" has become an integral part of even political journalism. When we see spectacle, though, we should ask ourselves who is supposed to be lulled into comfortable passivity and who ultimately benefits.

Journalists are supposed to have a vested interest in afflicting the comfortable and the powerful, but in today's climate they have a vested interest in keeping the powerful in comfort - and in power. This interest is personal, as Steinert describes, because of all the personal benefits they get, but also professional because they work for large corporations which have political and economic ties to the current power structures.

The manner in which "journalists" (it's hard to apply this label seriously to most of those in the profession these days) have become reliant upon the powerful was made evident in the political campaign on behalf of John G. Roberts' nomination to the Supreme Court, as US News explains:

When John G. Roberts is approved as chief justice of the United States, as expected, he can thank President Bush 's "Friends & Allies" program, which went to work on him immediately after he was nominated. The project, started by the Republican National Committee in the 2004 re-election campaign, is simple and effective: Give opinion makers, media friends, and even cocktail party hosts insider info on the topic of the day. How? Through E-mailed talking points, called D.C. Talkers, and conference calls.

For Roberts, it worked this way: A daily conference call to about 80 pundits, GOP-leaning radio and TV hosts, and newsmakers was made around 9 a.m. On the other end were the main Roberts gunslingers like Steve Schmidt at the White House and Ken Mehlman and Brian Jones at the RNC. D.C. Talkers would then be distributed to an even larger list filled with positive info about Roberts and lines of attack on his critics. "The idea," said one of those involved, "is to feed them information and have them invested in us." It has even created addicts, he added. "Now they come to us before going on TV."

So, "journalists" and pundits are taking their cues from and following the lead of the political power brokers who seek to have stories spun in a very particular way. If reporters don't play along, they lose access to the information being provided and risk being out-done by rivals. Therefore, in order to continue, they perceive a need to allow themselves to be led by the nose; in doing so, however, they fail to do their real job, which is to be an independent witness to what the politically powerful are doing.

Even Dan Rather recognizes that things have gotten pretty bad:

> *Addressing the Fordham University School of Law in Manhattan, occasionally forcing back tears, he said that in the intervening years [since Watergate, when reporters were more protected from political pressures], politicians "of every persuasion" had gotten better at applying pressure on the conglomerates that own the broadcast networks. He called it a "new journalism order."*

He said this pressure -- along with the "dumbed-down, tarted-up" coverage, the advent of 24-hour cable competition and the chase for ratings and demographics -- has taken its toll on the news business. "All of this creates a bigger atmosphere of fear in newsrooms," Rather said.

Rather was accompanied by HBO Documentary and Family president Sheila Nevins, both of whom were due to receive lifetime achievement awards at the News and Documentary Emmy Awards on Monday evening.

Nevins said that even in the documentary world, there's a certain kind of intimidation brought to bear these days, particularly from the religious right. "If you made a movie about (evolutionary biologist Charles) Darwin now, it would be revolutionary," Nevins said. "If we did a documentary on Darwin, I'd get a thousand hate e-mails."

So-called journalists are engaging in what is a mere illusion of journalism; in reality, they are engaging in little more than rewriting press releases on behalf of powerful interest groups. One way or another, they are doing more to reinforce traditional assumptions, stereotypes, and power structures than they are to challenge the status quo, ask hard questions, and encourage greater popular participation in the democratic system.

It's no wonder that the public isn't taking the news media very seriously anymore and regards comedians like Jon Stewart to be more reliable sources of news and information. As a comedian, he actually has a vested interest in challenging those in power rather than reinforcing their legitimacy. That used to be the job description of mainstream journalism.

One consequence of this incestuous relationship is that the role of the people is marginalized, if not forgotten altogether. Instead of being made to think, they are made to think that they are thinking. False controversies are presented in place of the real ones; the range of possible choices in any given issue is narrowed to include only those which the powerful political and economic interests have pre-determined; contradictory information is left out; dissenting voices are ignored as if they didn't exist at all.

BIBLIOGRAPHY

Black, Jay: *Mixed News: The Public/Civic/Communitarian Journalism Debate,* Mahwah, NJ: Lawrence Erlbaum, 1997.

Bliss, Edward: *Now the News: The Story of Broadcast Journalism,* New York, Columbia University Press, 1991.

Briggs, Asa and Peter Burke: *A Social History of the Media from Gutenberg to the Internet,* Malden, Blackwell, 2001.

Callahan, Christopher: *A Journalist's Guide to the Internet,* Boston, Allyn and Bacon, 2002.

Cannadine, David: *History and the Media,* New York, Palgrave Macmillian, 2004.

Carey, James W.: *Public Opinion and the Communication of Consent,* New York: Guilford Publications, 1995.

Clark, Roy Peter and G. Stuart Adam: *Journalism: The Democratic Craft,* New York, Oxford, 2006

Crowley, David. J. and Paul Heyer: *Communication in History,* Boston, Allyn and Bacon, 2003.

De Wolk, Roland: *Introduction to Online Journalism,* Boston, Allyn & Bacon, 2001.

Earl, R.: *Writing for Mass Communication,* White Plains, NY: Longman, 1996.

Ehrlich, Matthew C. *Journalism in the Movies.* Urbana: University of Illinois Press, 2004.

Eiseman, Leatrice: *Pantone Guide to Communicating with Color,* Cincinnati, North Light, 2000.

Frank, Reuven: *Out of Thin Air: The Brief Wonderful Life of Network News,* New York, Simon & Schuster, 1991.

George M. Killenberg: *The Conversation of Journalism: Communication, Community, and News,* Westport, CT: Praeger, 1994.

Graber, Doris A.: *Processing the News,* N.Y., Longman, 1984.

Hudson, Robert V.: *Mass Media,* New York, Garland Publishing, 1987.

Hutchison, Earl R.: *Writing for Mass Communication,* White Plains, NY: Longman, 1996.

Kolodzy, Janet: *Convergence Journalism: Writing and Reporting Across the News Media,* Llanham, MD: Rowman & Littlefield, 2006.

Langman, Larry: *The Media in the Movies,* Jefferson, NC: McFarland & Company, 1997.

Nora Paul: *Behind the Message: Information Strategies for Communicators,* Boston, Allyn & Bacon, 2004.

Robert W. Snyder: *Defining Moments in Journalism,* New Brunswick, NJ: Transaction Publishers, 1998.

Ross, Lillian: *Reporting Back: Notes on Journalism,* Washington, DC: Counterpoint, 2002.

Sachsman, David B.: *The Civil War and the Press,* New Brunswick, NJ: Transaction Publishers, 2000.

Sims, Norman: *Literary Journalism in the Twentieth Century,* New York, Oxford University Press, 1990.

Sloan, W. David: *Perspectives on Mass Communication History,* Hillsdale, NJ: Lawrence Erlbaum, 1991.

Startt, James D. and W. David Sloan: *Historical Methods in Mass Communication,* Hillsdale, NJ: Lawrence Erlbaum, 1989.

Streitmatter, Rodger: *Mightier Than the Sword: How the News Media Have Shaped American History,* Boulder, CO: Westview Press, 1997.

Suggs, Henry Lewis: *The Black Press in the Middle West, 1865-1985,* Westport, CT: Greenwood Press, 1996.

INDEX